what folks are saying about
What Lies Beneath

"*What Lies Beneath* reveals how 'natural' disasters like Katrina are increasingly man-made and caused by corporate greed, how those who have no role in creating climate chaos bear its worst burden, and how those involved in the crime of climate catastrophes use the disasters they have created to dispossess the poor, women, and people of color in the name of a 'cleanup.' But most importantly it brings us the voices of those whose lives were destroyed and who, against all odds, are rebuilding their lives and their communities. The determination to live is the highest form of resistance and struggle in times of dispensability and extermination. And it is this struggle that the testimonies in this book will not allow us to forget."

—**vandana shiva**, *Earth Democracy*

"*What Lies Beneath* is a work of fury, spawned not by the inchoate forces of nature, but by activists, poets, organizers, and scholars. This brilliant little book is a written response to the forces of state, corporate, and media power which converged to isolate, demonize, destroy, and finally, forget those many black and poor people who found themselves bitterly alone in the aftermath of Hurricane Katrina. Using voices which would rarely pierce the quasi-apartheid media cubicles, those who lived or worked there converge in this text to break the profound racial and class silence.

What Lies Beneath features many voices of women, many women of color, many of whom were among those least able to escape the natural, political, and economic carnage that was Katrina. Yet, *What Lies Beneath* is far more than a mourning saga. It is an indictment of the social-political systems that made Katrina a certainly waiting to happen. It is an analysis of why it happened, why it happened where it happened, and why it is an historic marker of things to come."

—**mumia abu jamal**, *Live from Death Row*

"*What Lies Beneath* is a book that will keep alive the memory of one of the most dramatic and terrible events of the new millenium—the catastrophe of the Katrina hurricane, and its aftermath. The writers come at the event from many different vantage points, but they all probe deeply into those fateful weeks, pointing us to the larger significance of the disaster and the reactions to it. At the center of the story are the unavoidable issues of race, class, and the shameful callousness of officialdom. This book will keep us thinking for a long time about what happened, why it happened, and provoke us to examine honestly the nature of the society in which we live."

—**howard zinn**, *A People's History of the United States*

"The suffering that continues in the aftermath of Hurricane Katrina is not accidental. It results from years of intentional, planned wrong doing committed by powerful economic and political interests. Future human-made disasters will only be prevented if the prophetic voices presented in *What Lies Beneath* are heeded."

—**margaret kimberley**, Freedom Rider blog

"We never know enough about our enemies. That's why they do so well. Katrina was a cover and an exposer of Bush Fascism . This book helps us understand this. Understand or die!"

—**amiri baraka**, *Tales of the Out & the Gone*

"This volume is wide-ranging in style as it narrows in on its subject—the truth about race in the United States that is revealed in the events around Hurricane Katrina. The combination of on-the-ground reporting and analysis placing events in the wider context helps readers untangle the way in which race, gender, and class affected the outcome of that most unnatural disaster. The book bristles with the anger we all should feel, and offers the critical self-reflection we all should engage in.

—**robert jensen**, *The Heart of Whiteness*

WHAT LIES BENEATH
Katrina, Race, and the State of the Nation

EDITED BY THE SOUTH END PRESS COLLECTIVE

south end press
cambridge, massachusetts

The views expressed in the book belong to the authors and
not the institutions with which they are affiliated.

A portion of the proceeds will be donated to the **People's
Hurricane Relief Fund and Oversight Coalition.**

Cover design: **Design Action Collective.**

Photo credit: **AP Images/Bill Haber.** "New Orleans residents walk
through floodwaters that besiege the Crescent City on Tuesday,
Aug. 30, 2005. Hurricane Katrina devastated the Louisiana
and Mississippi coasts when it came ashore on Monday."

Interior cover images: **Ricardo Levins Morales/Northland Poster.
Collective.** Inside front, "Katrina" and inside back, "Reconstruction."

Page design and production: **South End Press Collective/
Joey Fox** using **Adobe InDesign CS2.**

Library of Congress Cataloging-in-Publication Data
What lies beneath : Katrina, race, and the state of the nation.
  p. cm.
Includes bibliographical references and index.
ISBN–13: 978–0–89608–767–5 (pbk. : alk. paper)
ISBN–10: 0–89608–767–0 (pbk.)
  1. Hurricane Katrina, 2005--Social aspects. 2. Disaster relief--Social
aspects--Louisiana--New Orleans. 3. Marginality, Social
--Louisiana--New Orleans. 4. People with social disabilities--
Government policy--United States. 5. New Orleans (La.)--Race
relations. 6. United States--Race relations. I. South End Press.
HV6362005.N4 W43 2007
976.3'35064--dc22
          2006033608

Printed with **union labor** in Canada on **acid-free, recycled paper.**
10 09 08 07   1 2 3 4 5 6 7 8 9

South End Press
7 Brookline Street, #1
Cambridge, MA 02139

http://www.southendpress.org
southend@southendpress.org

read. write. revolt.

contents

preface

up from the depths
south end press collective

"In all these struggles we must be assertive and challenging, combating the deep-seated tendency in Americans to be liberal, that is, to evade struggling over questions of principle for fear of creating tensions or becoming unpopular. Instead we must live by the fundamental dialectical principle: that progress comes only from struggling to resolve contradictions."

—anonymously-authored feminist pamphlet, (1976).
Quoted in Ain't I a Woman, *bell hooks (1981)*

In August 2005, thousands of New Orleans and other US Gulf region residents—overwhelmingly poor, overwhelmingly people of color, the majority black—were left on their own to face one of the worst "natural" disasters in US history. As Katrina's waters receded and the body count soared, an ugly truth (re)surfaced: the lives of those who are poor, who are vulnerable, and who are not white are not valued by the US government. And so, those with no means to escape were implored to pray and then blamed. And so, survivors were criminalized as "looters" for struggling to obtain food, water, diapers, medicine, and other essentials of life that no one else could or would provide. And so, they were left to die in prisons, in nursing homes, and on the street.

In the immediate aftermath of the storm, a levee of a different sort was breached as corporate media sharply rebuked the Bush administration in a manner unprecedented in the post-9/11 era. Across the political spectrum, commentators and celebrities alike chimed in, outraged that the US government would let this happen to Americans, even "those Americans."

Many expressed genuine concern with the fate of those affected by the hurricane and, more pointedly, government malfeasance. But quickly "the story" devolved into something else, where the reality of tremendous human suffering and ecological devastation was eclipsed by the scandal of revelation itself: the image of an American city looking "like a third world country" for everyone to see. But covering "the story" obscures the millions outside of New Orleans living without clean air and water; without decent education, housing, nutrition, health care, and work; without freedom from police brutality and state repression; and the thousands deported, displaced, and dying in prisons and illegal wars from coast to coast, Gulf to Gulf.

What Lies Beneath rests on the premise that Hurricane Katrina mirrors with terrible poignancy the state of a nation—a damning and bitterly accurate portrait of everyday life in America. Despite a chorus of claims to the contrary, Hurricane Katrina was not an equal opportunity disaster. Its asymmetrical impact on people's lives vis-à-vis their relative place within the matrix of oppression cannot be denied. If your life was hard before the hurricane, it was exponentially harder during and after the storm—and remains so *up to this day*. For those who suffer daily the existing, pervasive, and insidious social inequities that are the US reality, Katrina was not an anomaly. It was simply business as usual.

We at the South End Press knew there would be a deluge of books in the wake of the storm—most of them marginalizing or depoliticizing race, focusing on the narrative of government failure. For this reason, the collective decided to leverage our power as political publishers and reassert a more radical agenda: let the people who have survived and helped and agitated speak for themselves. What follows is a powerful assembly of jurists heralding a collective demand for justice in their daily determination for a world where no one will ever again "die of thirst while surrounded by water."

introduction

below the water line
kalamu ya salaam

New Orleans is situated three feet below sea level and surrounded by water—Lake Pontchartrain to the north, the Mississippi River to the south. The river snakes around in a lazy S and forms a bowl within which most of the city sits. All around the city are marshland and swamps. Canals, lagoons, and bayous permeate the landscape. Levees and pumps work to protect the city and keep it dry. Water is the lifeblood of New Orleans—its role as a port city, connecting the American interior to the world, has guaranteed its national and worldwide status for more than two centuries.

Hurricanes, semitropical storms, and floods have been a threat to the city since its founding in 1718. The great Mississippi River flood of 1927 threatened to inundate the city. Fortunately, levee breaks much further upriver spared the city, even though the powers that be decided, unnecessarily, to breech the river levee above New Orleans in St. Bernard Parish. Spike Lee's movie *When The Levees Broke* contains historic footage of the dynamiting of the levee. In 1965, Hurricane Betsy flooded the Lower Ninth Ward section of New Orleans, which is directly adjacent to St. Bernard Parish. Lesser threats have been perennial, with all kinds of woeful predictions about the big one yet to come.

We've had numerous close calls in the last few decades but the eye of the storm would invariably miss us, usually turning at the last minute and making landfall to the east of the city. We'd often receive heavy rains and temporary flooding that dissipated in a day or two. Everybody knew to stock up on water, canned food, batteries, candles, and other provisions to carry you through a short period without power and city services. Hell, we'd even hold hurricane parties to wait for the storm to hit or miss us.

That's the way life in New Orleans had always gone.

When Hurricane Ivan threatened in 2004, there was a voluntary evacuation. More than 5,000 people sought refuge in the Louisiana Superdome. Although the storm missed us, as usual, there were major problems at the Superdome, crowd control and inadequate provisions among them. The city administration promised there would never again be a breakdown like what happened at the Superdome.

In late August 2005, Hurricane Katrina missed the city. Once again we had been spared. It was business as usual until…the levees broke and Mr. Go deluged the eastern portion of the city. Mr. Go is the Mississippi River Gulf Outlet (MRGO), a man-made canal constructed in the mid-60s by the Army Corps of Engineers that runs a direct 70-mile course from the Industrial Canal in New Orleans to the nearby Gulf of Mexico. Most of America is aware of the levee breaches that flooded the east bank of New Orleans, but few are aware of Mr. Go, which ran through St. Bernard Parish and the area of New Orleans known as "the East." St. Bernard Parish was totally flooded and the East, which contained approximately 40 percent of the city's population, was extensively flooded. An estimated 80,000 residences were flooded in New Orleans. Every building in St. Bernard Parish received floodwaters. This flooding was not directly caused by the storm, but rather was the result of levee failures and poor or nonexistent flood prevention made worse by depletion of the wetlands surrounding the city.

The resulting destruction had been predicted, and flood prevention plans had been drawn up. But these were systematically ignored by the federal government, which cut the Army Corps of Engineers' budget, year after year. Meanwhile, petroleum companies were given tax breaks and allowed to cut canals throughout southeast Louisiana. These canals injected salt water into an ecosystem of freshwater marshes, killing off the flora that held the land together, which resulted in erosion.

Proposals to stem erosion, improve the levees, and build up the marshes were deemed too expensive. Compared with the costs, thus far, of dealing with what is commonly viewed as Katrina's destruction, the cost of the preventive proposals would have been minor. At the heart of the refusal to deal with preventive proposals is a government in flat-out denial about environmental issues. Ross Gelbspan is correct in his indictment: "To be sure, countless extreme weather events have occurred over the past 10,000 years. But the increasing frequency and intensity of prolonged droughts, downpours, heat waves, and storms is indisputably a signature of the early stages of global warming."

That's the physical landscape. The political landscape must also be understood. From the Carolinas to Texas and Oklahoma, New Orleans was the only blue spot in an otherwise solidly red landscape. Not only had New Orleans voted overwhelmingly against President Bush, New Orleans also ensured that a Democrat was elected governor in a very close race, and that a Democrat was elected senator in a similarly tight race. Although the city's mayor, Ray Nagin, is nominally a Democrat, he supported the Republican candidate for the governorship and also won reelection with the support of Republicans. These political considerations are not negligible and must be taken into consideration in making any analysis of post-Katrina conditions and activities in New Orleans.

Even in New Orleans much of this background is unknown to people who are wondering why it's taking so long to get New Orleans back on its feet. Moreover, given a paucity of information in the mass media, it's no surprise that many people across the country assume the reconstruction of New Orleans is proceeding at a steady pace.

This is the backdrop that *What Lies Beneath: Katrina, Race, and the State of the Nation* attempts to penetrate—through testimony, reflection, and analysis.

Poet Suheir Hammad, who is of Palestinian background, sensitively notes:

> I do not wish
> To place words in living mouths
> Or bury the dead dishonorably
>
> I am not deaf to cries escaping shelters
> That citizens are not refugees
> Refugees are not Americans

She has fingered the national shame that CNN, and other media networks, broadcast worldwide: Were the sufferers who we all saw really American citizens, and if they were, was nothing being done to help them?

Over and over, this question is asked. Even those who were suffering could not believe that they were in America, on television, suffering and with no help forthcoming. Thus, in her statement, Mandy Carter declares:

> I asked myself how it is that we can be the richest country in the world and we can't get help into New Orleans and the other Gulf Coast states affected by Katrina. We then heard reports that many of the National Guard units that would have normally been called up in this situation were not available because they were stationed in Iraq. And to add insult to injury, how is it that we can deploy US troops all the way across the world within days, yet we can't get them down into Louisiana, Mississippi, and Alabama?

Implicit in Carter's questions is the belief that the capability existed to deal with the situation but there was no political will to do so. To the degree that we believe in American freedom, justice, and democracy, the lack of response by the government is not understandable. Tiffany Brown is flabbergasted:

> Hasn't the event of the hurricane, storm surge, and the fate of the forgotten and stranded highlighted the plight of the poor? Hasn't it highlighted the underlying racism and classism that exists in this country? Where are the individuals asking questions about who is getting the rebuilding jobs? Where are the individuals asking questions about what happened to the millions of dollars collected

in the name of Katrina survivors by various charitable organizations? Where is the outrage that spurs
us as a nation into action?

Although I understand and accept the legitimacy of these
testimony viewpoints, I think, influenced by the portrait presented by the news media, many, many people misunderstand
the magnitude of the destruction. Lewis Lapham's summation
is a prime example: "As it became increasingly evident that the
storm had inflicted its heaviest damage on people who were poor,
illiterate, and predominantly black, what emerged from the
Mississippi mud was the ugly recognition of the United States
as a society divided against itself across the frontiers of race and
class."

The deeper truth is that all strata of the black community
was wiped out by the flooding. New Orleans East was largely
populated by black homeowners, the majority of whom were
college-educated professionals. The East was also dotted with
gated communities and enclaves that housed the overwhelming
majority of the wealthiest sector of the black community. These
medical and legal professionals—upper-level civil servants,
teachers and professors, entrepreneurs and athletes, contractors and clergy—lost their businesses, churches, and residences.
Those who had nothing, lost everything. Those who had everything, lost everything. The social fabric was torn beyond repair.

CNN showed us the fate of those stranded atop roofs, but
what about the cardiologist whose office—which housed over $1
million of medical equipment and served over 7,000 patients—
was totally destroyed and whose two-story $300,000 home was
flooded? And what about the college professor who no longer has
a job but still has a mortgage, a car note, and children's tuition
to pay? Most black professionals have established themselves
in other cities, have enrolled their children into better schools,
and are using whatever insurance money they receive to sustain
themselves as they transition from New Orleans to wherever.
They cannot afford to return.

Unfortunately, there is no voice in this collection representing black professionals. Nevertheless, the major culprit is easy to identify once we move beyond a victim fixation. Independent journalist Jordan Flaherty, who has been a consistent New Orleans-based critical voice, precisely notes: "New Orleans was not devastated by a hurricane. The damage came from decades of brutal negligence, deficient planning, and from a stunningly slow response on the part of a local, state, and federal government that didn't care about the people of New Orleans, and still doesn't."

The strongest sections of *What Lies Beneath* are contained in the reflections and analysis of activists and organizers struggling to make change in New Orleans. The major focus is on Common Ground Relief, a collective that has been organizing volunteer relief and recovery work. Although Common Ground Relief is not the only volunteer organization working in New Orleans, it is the largest and most visible effort and is doubly important because it is a true initiative of "the people" rather than a government or professional charity initiative.

Roger Benham's perspective as a medical volunteer who is also an activist forthrightly raises questions that are often debated throughout New Orleans:

> There have been problems and limitations. No matter how hard we worked or how many donations we received, our efforts could never match the lack of effort on the part of the government. It was sometimes easy to become intoxicated with how much was accomplished with so little, but we should be realistic. We cannot perform helicopter rescues, evacuate large numbers of people, or deal with thousands of hospital patients and nursing home residents, as the official response did in the first days of September, however belatedly or badly. We cannot build levees that can withstand storm surges, or restore wetlands that have been lost, and which would have provided additional protection. These are all larger social functions that require the mobilization of large-scale resources. We cannot, in some separate activist milieu, deal with the national problem of racism that Katrina

showed to all of us. Racism is something we are constantly called upon to deal with in our smaller community as well. In the months after the storm, it became a problem that so many predominantly white activists were able to flock to New Orleans to work, while so many black New Orleanians did not have the means to do so and remained stranded in their diaspora. Many community activists from Louisiana became frustrated with the privilege and ignorance exhibited by volunteers who came from outside the state. Some might view our initial response in September as the beginning of this dynamic.

Sue Hilderbrand and her Common Ground Relief colleagues go a step further and ask the tough question:

> Common Ground Relief's founders originally assumed that the presence of outside relief volunteers, predominantly young, white, and middle-class, would be short-term. Assistance from outsiders would be needed only until a critical mass of predominantly black and low-income residents could return to the city. However, even a year after the disaster, historically neglected neighborhoods, such as the Lower Ninth Ward, remain without electricity, water, and basic city services, leaving local people with little to return to. As a result, what started as a disaster relief effort by a small group has evolved into a sustained effort of outsider volunteers, with the unanswered question of "When is it time to leave?"

This question points directly to a tension that the women of INCITE! Women of Color Against Violence courageously address. If volunteers from outside New Orleans take a leading role in the recovery effort, what role is there for locally based activists and organizers? It's axiomatic that one should not slap the hand that helps us, but...This is a difficult "but" to address, and we should be extremely grateful for INCITE's analysis:

> Though hundreds of nonprofits, NGOs, university urban planning departments, and foundations have come through the city, they have paid little attention to the organizing led by people of color that existed before Katrina and that is struggling now more than ever. A look at who and what gets

funding from foundations to support work in New
Orleans reveals the priorities of these foundations
and the entire nonprofit system. Organizations that
represent their work through quick and quantifiable accomplishments are rewarded by the system.
Foundations are not only drawn to them but are
pressured by their own donors to fund them.

INCITE! is not indicting Common Ground, but rather
questioning the whole social landscape of recovery and reconstruction in post–Katrina New Orleans. Over one year later and most of
the federal recovery money has not yet arrived into the city.

Inaction at the federal level has hamstrung state efforts
and reduced local government to begging. At the same time New
Orleans is ground zero for urban planners nationwide. We are suffering the whiplash of being ignored by the federal powers that
be while being minutely scrutinized and experimented with by
planners and professionals representing moneyed interests ranging
from major foundations and think tanks to multinational corporations and reemergent carpetbaggers.

Some people argue that there is no realistic plan for recovery
just as there was no real evacuation plan. In both cases, I believe
the absence of a plan was the plan. For example, close to 60 percent
of New Orleans residents were renters. Since the storm, rents have
doubled and even tripled. More than 5,000 pre–Katrina HUD
housing units are shuttered and scheduled for demolition. HUD
promised 1,000 units would be available by August 2006. There
has been no movement. There is no housing available for the working poor.

The worst is yet to come. FEMA-subsidized housing for
more than 200,000 exiled New Orleanians is scheduled to come
to a screeching halt after 18 months, in February 2007. Where will
these people go? What will they do? The general consensus is that
many of them will return home to be homeless.

Jared Sexton closes this book by asking a vital question and
pointing out the need for a deeper analysis. Sexton situates his
question in the context of an examination of the book *Covenant
With Black America*, a collection of essays edited by Tavis Smiley.

The sentiment of timely expediency proffered by the CWBA—a solemn promise to "stop talking and start doing," based on a belief that "actions speak louder than words"—plays to an understandably popular urgency that emanates quite directly from the rigors of everyday survival faced by the vast majority of black people in the United States and, not incidentally, from the continued material precariousness and acute status anxiety of the black middle class. However, I submit that, in point of fact, "we who are dark" have done precious little talking about our pain in this post–civil rights era and probably a bit too much posturing about our plans. If anything, we have a surplus of plans, many of them quite sound and long-standing and unrealized. What we do not have is a language, much less a political culture, that adequately addresses the complexity of our position(s), our predicament(s), and our pain(s) without recourse to euphemism.

Sexton concludes on a hopeful note with a discussion of Eric Mann's book, *Katrina's Legacy: White Racism and Black Reconstruction in New Orleans and the Gulf Coast*, which was based on his widely circulated "Letter in Support of the Movement in New Orleans and the Gulf Coast,"

In order to situate the event of Hurricane Katrina squarely within the afterlife of slavery, Mann discusses the prospect of a radical redevelopment plan under the heading of a Third Reconstruction, one drawing upon the dynamic arc of the first (1865–1877) and second (1955–1975) historic iterations. If, he argues, the modern civil rights and black liberation movements sought to refashion the postbellum project anatomized so brilliantly by DuBois, then perhaps this early–21st century effort, spreading out along the pathways of dispersal from the epicenter of the crisis, may yet re-ignite the best of those "two decades of the sixties" that shook US society—and the global system it continues to dominate—to its foundation.

Sexton's language is that of the academy, but the thrust of his thinking is revolutionary. The next step is figuring out how to translate these sentiments into a common vernacular, and then moving from planning to action. Sexton is right to emphasize the need for language, which is another way of calling for an appropriate analysis. Any and every movement requires committed individuals, ideas, and institutions.

Some of us continue to believe we need a revolution, a complete change in the ruling social order. Progressives across the country have responded to the Katrina disaster not only as volunteers but also in hopes of establishing focal points of organizational development. The truth is, however, that a disaster is not a revolution.

The most successful organizers in this period are those who engage in deep work within specific sectors while simultaneously analyzing conditions and planning for change.

The INCITE! organizers and the Common Ground organizers are examples of those doing deep work, examples of those who are asking critical questions of themselves and their circumstances while engaging in day-to-day efforts to meet the needs of people who have been affected by the twin disaster of flood and government failure. There are others in New Orleans and across the Gulf South, many of them doing extremely important work in virtual anonymity—they are seldom featured on television.

Ultimately, whether highlighted or ignored, there is no substitute for face-to-face organizing around the needs of people within specific conditions. Moreover, it is critical that this struggle be a dynamic of praxis, a constant evaluation and realignment of thought and practice within the context of day-to-day assessment. What worked and why, what didn't work and why? The need for deep struggle is the ultimate lesson this book teaches.

Only deep work will bring about real social change rather than just a cosmetic repair of an inequitable status quo. On-the-ground work and honest, critical study, guided by dreams and revolutionary principles, this is the only recipe for success.

We who live below the water line have no choice. Our first priority is to survive. Our second priority is to struggle. Our ultimate responsibility is to win. Survive. Struggle. Win. This book is a record of these efforts.

a raging flood of tears
ewuare osayande

they are pulling our dead out of the dead water now

they are pulling our dead out of the dead water now
like they pulled Till out of the Tallahatchie River
and even if we did place the blame where it belongs
would they get off like the men who murdered Emmett?

while reporters blamed us for staying
refusing to see the chains that tied us to the catastrophe
that was to come
like when they tied Malcolm Little's dad
to the tracks
and left him for dead
cause they knew the train was coming

they knew the flood was coming
they knew the levees would break
they were warned
but did nothing
they were warned
but did nothing

they refused to prepare

they are pulling our dead out of the dead water now
counting them as if they were tallying votes
but you cannot measure disgrace with a body count

and no one wins in death

what have we now but our heartbeats?
and tears
and the whys
of our questions keep coming

even Jesus was said
to have fed the poor
with a few fish and some bread
should we not expect more
from the richest nation
in the history of the world?

scabs are being ripped away
like the homes
revealing old wounds
bleeding sores
infected by the toxic scum
of lies we ingest

as the media contrived words to describe the people
when for five days they were treated like slaves

time warped to the days of whips, chains
and names that were not our own

slave ship screams

ancestors haunt in their hollers for help
in front of cameras that don't care
sending an SOS of sorrow
to a world that looks on in pity and contempt

but hope doesn't stop hunger
and faith can't quench a thirst
mouths parched in the parish
surrounded by water

but can't take a drink

yes, this is hell

the smell of rotting flesh and feces
the stench of death
like bush's breath hot with deceit
burning under a louisiana sun
merciless as a slave master
hysterical heat

gnashing teeth, bleeding gums
and the children
the babies delirious with grief

and still they were trapped by the help that would come
abandoned by rescue teams on Highway 10

the help that didn't help
the help that held them hostage
at convention centers that became concentration camps

no refuge
no refuge
no refuge
for the women and their children
and the elders dying in their wheel chairs

smuggled to the super dome that became the prison
at Abu Ghraib
blindfolded by the darkness
and tortured due to the ineptitude of officials
sinking in a cess pool of paranoia
held hostage by helplessness

how long did it take Africans
in texas to learn that they were free?

we know how slow the government can be
when it comes to we
who are Black and poor

families again severed
like before
when the auction block was swollen with our blood and tears
the years are of no consequence

and now we wander the country looking for wives and sons,
daughters and fathers, nanas, poppas, husbands and cousins
and lovers and friends and mothers and nieces, nephews and…

tracing the scent of love in hope of embracing them again
on this side

pouring through web pages
hoping to notice a name that sounds like happiness
watching the tv
hoping to recognize a face
that resembles our own

looking for family

longing for home

and I can hear Nina Simone singing
"Mississippi Goddamn Blues"
we who picked cotton there
grew families out of the very ground
we never owned
sucked down gristle just to survive
raised God out the dust bowl
and blew life into our bodies
with nothing
nothing
nothing
but the defiant desire to live

and once more nothing is all we have
but the defiant desire to live again

resurrected like the Jeez that is us

who will march a jazz dirge
on down Bourbon Street
to honor those whose bodies still float in the Ninth Ward?

who will rebuild the city
that city of saints and haints?
bring the reconstruction that never came after lee surrendered
the war

jim crow knows
let trent lott rot in the rubble of his plantation mansion
for all those that perished unnecessarily

yes there is anger
a raging flood of tears

bush looted our taxes
sent them overseas
robbed our rights
cracked presidential jokes as the smoke still rose

"the soft bigotry of low expectations" is bush's to claim
a smug racism he learned on his mother's knee

yes the US is a Third World nation
no corporate press can cover the truth now
where dictators lie, cheat and steal
then kill the poor that would defy them

the emperor has no clothes
his ass is exposed
been stripped naked by his own shame
time to name names

there is a raging flood headed right to the White House

and FEMA can't rescue you now

what has happened here is a crime
the homicide of an entire city

hear the prophecy my ancestors sung

God showed Noah
by the rainbow sign
said it won't be water but fire next time

the flames are burning!

slum clearance
lewis h. lapham

The comfort of the rich rests upon an abundance of the poor.

—Voltaire

On Monday, August 29, a category [3] hurricane slammed into New Orleans with winds reaching [127] miles an hour, and by Thursday, September 1, the city looked just about the way a doomed city is supposed to look according to the Book of Revelation. Which, given the faith-based political theory currently in office in Washington, should have surprised nobody. For the last 30 years the scribes and Pharisees allied with the several congregations of both the radical and the reactionary right have been preaching the lesson that government is a sink of iniquity—by definition inefficient, unjust, wasteful, and corrupt, a mess of lies deserving neither the trust nor the affection of true Americans. True Americans place their faith in individual initiative, moral virtue, and personal responsibility, knowing in their hearts that government is the enemy of the people, likely to do more harm than good.

So it proved in New Orleans during the first week of September. At every level of officialdom—city, parish, state, and federal—the tribunes of the people met the standard of bureaucratic futility and criminal negligence imputed to them by two generations of Republican publicists, and within the few days before, during, and after the hurricane's arrival, they managed to facilitate the loss of life, liberty, and property for several hundred thousand of their fellow citizens. The devastation fell somewhat short of the biblical prophecy—no blood in the sea, the floodwaters unsmitten with the bloom of Wormwood, no angels overhead armed with the trumpets of Woe; even so, despite the absence of giant locusts wearing breastplates of iron, about as satisfactory a result as could be hoped for from a government public-works program—the storm warnings ignored or discredited, the levees in a reliably shoddy state of repair, 1 million people left homeless in the mostly uninsured wreckage scattered across 90,000 square miles in four states, dead animals drifting in the New Orleans sewage and rotting on the beaches of Biloxi, the sick and elderly dying of thirst in the stench and heat of the Superdome, poisonous snakes making the rounds of hospital emergency rooms, rats gnawing at the corpses of the drowned.

Even more impressive than the scale of the calamity was the laissez-faire response of the government officials who understood that it was not their place to question, much less attempt to interfere with, an act of God. When confronted with scenes of anguish that might have tempted overly emotional public servants to ill-considered activisms, the Department of Homeland Security held fast to the policy of principled restraint. Spendthrift liberals rush to help people who refuse to help themselves; prudent conservatives know that such efforts smack of socialism. The residents of New Orleans had been told to evacuate the city before the hurricane came ashore, and if they didn't do so, well, whose fault was that? Government cannot be held responsible for the behavior of people who don't follow instructions, aren't mature enough to carry an American Express card or drive an SUV.

Every now and then, of course, government must show concern for the country's less fortunate citizens—the gesture is deemed polite in societies nominally democratic—and two days after the flooding submerged most of New Orleans under as much as 15 feet of foul and stagnant water, President George W. Bush graciously cut short his Texas vacation to gaze upon the ruined city from the height of 2,500 feet. Air Force One remained overhead for 35 whole minutes, which was long enough to impress upon the President the comparison to a big-budget Hollywood disaster movie. To the White House aides-de-camp aboard the plane he was reported to have said, "It's devastating, it's got to be doubly devastating on the ground." A sensitive observation, indicating that he had noticed something seriously amiss—small houses floating in the water, big boats moored in trees. A president crippled by too active an imagination might have made the mistake of wanting to see for himself the devastation on the ground, possibly even going so far as to say a few words to the evacuees in the Superdome. But the newscasts were loud with rumors of armed gangs of unattractive black people looting convenience stores and raping infant girls, and if one or more of the mobs happened to incite a riot, the liberal news media would publish unpleasant photographs and draw unpatriotic conclusions. Better to wait until the army had set up a secure perimeter.

By Friday, September 2, four days after the hurricane made landfall, enough military units were in place to allow the President to upgrade the demonstration of his concern with the staging of resolute drop-bys in Louisiana, Mississippi, and Alabama. But if it was clear from his manner that he wished to convey sympathy and offer encouragement, it was also clear that he was at a loss to relate the words in the air to the "doubly devastating" death and destruction on the ground. Standing tall in shirtsleeves in front of the cameras in Mobile, he acknowledged the misfortune that had befallen his good friend Senator Trent Lott (R., Miss.):

> The good news is, and it's hard for some to see it now—that out of this chaos is going to come a fantastic Gulf Coast, like it was before. Out of the rubbles of Trent Lott's house—he's lost his entire house—there's going to be a fantastic house, and I'm looking forward to sitting on the porch.

Later that same day, departing from the airport in New Orleans, the President hit the note of solemnly conservative compassion appropriate to an HBO production of the decline and fall of Rome: "You know, I'm going to fly out of here in a minute, but I want you to know that I'm not going to forget what I've seen."

Most of the other government spokespersons within range of a microphone during the first week in September might as well have been relaying their remarks by satellite from a map room in Bermuda. By Thursday, September 1, reports from the scene at the New Orleans Convention Center had been repeatedly broadcast on every network in the country—several thousand people without food or water, all of them desperate, quite a few of them dying. The news hadn't reached Michael Chertoff, director of the Department of Homeland Security in Washington, who had waited a judicious 36 hours after the storm's arrival before declaring it "an incident of national significance." To an interviewer from National Public Radio, Chertoff said, "I've not heard a report of thousands of people in the Convention Center who don't have food and water." The people in question presumably hadn't filled out the necessary forms. Nor had they informed Michael Brown, director of the Federal Emergency Management Agency, who also hadn't heard of any trouble at the Convention Center and who told Wolf Blitzer on September 1, "Considering the dire circumstances that we have in New Orleans, virtually a city that has been destroyed, things are going relatively well." Which was the preferred tone of voice throughout the rest of the week on the part of the Washington gentry doing their best to take an interest in people they neither knew nor wished to know.

Former First Lady Barbara Bush on September 5, reviewing the condition of the hurricane flood evacuees in the Houston Astrodome:

> What I'm hearing, which is sort of scary, is that they all want to stay in Texas. Everybody is so overwhelmed by the hospitality. And so many of the people in the arena here, you know, were underprivileged anyway, so this (*chuckle*) is working very well for them.

GOP strategist Jack Burkman, September 7:

> I understand there are 10,000 people dead. It's terrible. It's tragic. But in a democracy of 300 million people, over years and years and years, these things happen.

September 8, First Lady Laura Bush:

> I also want to encourage anybody who was affected by hurricane Corrina [*sic*] to make sure their children are in school.

House Majority Leader Tom DeLay, September 9, bucking up the spirits of three young hurricane evacuees from New Orleans at the Astrodome:

> Now tell me the truth, boys, is this kind of fun?

Earlier in the week Mrs. Bush might have been pardoned for mistaking the name of the hurricane—hurricanes come and go in the same way that summer disaster movies come and go, and only a bleeding heart leftist would expect the theatergoers in a Washington screening room to remember which is which—but by September 8 the news reports from New Orleans and points east were indicating an even more feckless government response than previously had been supposed—the USS *Bataan*, fully supplied with medical facilities, held at a safe distance offshore for reasons unexplained, National Guard units delayed in the confusions of bureaucratic move and countermove, the dysfunction of FEMA understood as the result of the nepotistic hiring of its senior management, trucks bringing ice and water rerouted to South Carolina, evacuees herded onto planes without being told where the planes were bound, the order to evacuate New Orleans made impractical by the simultaneous disappearance of the city's public transportation systems.

As it became increasingly evident that the storm had inflicted its heaviest damage on people who were poor, illiterate, and predominantly black, what emerged from the Mississippi mud was the ugly recognition of the United States as a society divided against itself across the frontiers of race and class. Not "one nation under God, indivisible, with liberty and justice for all" but two nations, divisible by bank account, with liberty and justice for those able to pay the going rate for a government pimp.

The unwelcome sight evoked angry shouts of Woe from all the trumpets of the news media—outraged editorials, harsh questions from television anchorpersons ordinarily as mild as milk, a rising tide of bitter reproach from politicians both Democratic and Republican. The abrupt decline in the President's approval ratings prompted his press agents to send him on a frenzied round of image refurbishment—Mr. Bush holding a press conference to accept responsibility for the federal government's storm-related failures, Mr. Bush at the National Cathedral in Washington, declaring a "National Day of Prayer and Remembrance," Mr. Bush back again on the Gulf Coast, posed in front of the stage-lit St. Louis Cathedral in New Orleans, promising to do and spend "what it takes" ($100 billion, maybe $200 billion) to restore "the passionate soul" of the dead city.

If the performances weren't as uplifting as the President might have hoped, the fault possibly was to be found in his inability to hide the fact of his genuine and irritated surprise. What was everybody complaining about, for God's sake? Who didn't know that America was divided into a nation of the rich and a nation of the poor? What else had every self-respecting Republican politician been doing for the last 30 years if not bending his or her best efforts to achieve that very purpose? Didn't anybody remember the words of the immortal Ronald Reagan's first inaugural address: "Government is not the so-lution to our problem; government is the problem"? Had everybody forgotten the noble question asked and answered in 1987 by Margaret Thatcher, that great and good British prime minister: "Who is society? There is no such thing! There are individual men and women; there are families"? Some families make it to higher ground; others don't. Such is the way of the world and the natural order of things, visible every day in the pictures from Africa on CNN. Why else was the Republican Party so popular—elected to the White House, put in charge of the Congress and the Supreme Court—if not to give to the haves and take from the have nots? It wasn't as if anybody, least of all President Bush, had made any secret of the project. All the major legislation passed by Congress over the last five years—the transportation bill, the Medicare prescription bill, the tax bills favoring corporations and wealthy individuals, the bankruptcy bill, etcetera—strengthens the power of money to limit and control the freedom of individuals. During the early weeks of September, when countless thousands of people on the Gulf Coast were sorely in need of rescue, Senator Bill Frist (R., Tenn.), the Republican majority leader in the Senate, never once lost sight of the more urgent rescue mission, which was to press forward the legislation intended to privatize Social Security and eliminate the estate tax. Senator Frist is a doctor but first and foremost a loyal Republican and a man who knows how to order his priorities—before the hand on the heart, the thumb on the coin.

As surprised as the President by the grumbling noises in the suddenly and uncharacteristically conscience-stricken media, a heavenly host of Republican preachers and politicians was quick to shift the story into the True American context of individual initiative, moral virtue, and personal responsibility. Thus Senator Rick Santorum (R., Pa.):

> I mean, you have people who don't heed those warnings and then put people at risk as a result of not heeding those warnings. There may be a need to look at tougher penalties on those who decide to ride it out and understand that there are consequences to not leaving.

Consequences also for not leading one's life in accordance with the instructions given in the Bible, the point made in the seconding of Senator Santorum's motion by numerous spokesmen for Christ. Thus the pastor of the New Covenant Fellowship of New Orleans: "New Orleans now is free of Southern Decadence, the sodomites, the witchcraft workers, false religion—it's free of all these things now." Or again, more subtly, by the Columbia Christians for Life. The organization

correlates storm tracks with cities harboring abortion clinics
and supplemented its press release referring to the five such
establishments in New Orleans with a satellite photograph that
"looks like a fetus facing to the left (west) in the womb, in the
early weeks of gestation."

Not a natural disaster, the hurricane, but a blessing in
disguise, so seen and much appreciated by the forward thinking parties of enlightened Republicanism. To the readers of
the *Wall Street Journal* on September 9, Congressman Richard
Baker (R., La.), brought the good news of a divinely inspired
slum clearance project. "We finally cleaned up public housing
in New Orleans," he said. "We couldn't do it, but God did."

As is well known and understood in the elevated circles
of Republican political thought, God helps those who help
themselves, and on September 13 *Time* magazine quoted an
unnamed White House source confirming the miracle of the
loaves and fishes soon to be visited upon the well-connected
servants of the Lord in Louisiana, Mississippi, and Alabama.
"Nothing can salve the wounds like money...you'll see a much
more aggressively engaged President, traveling to the Gulf
Coast a lot and sending a lot of people down there."

By the time it comes to writing next month's [*Harper's*]
Notebook, I expect that we'll have had the chance to count the
ways in which the master chefs of our indolent but nevertheless ravenous government can carve the body of Christ into the
sweetmeats of swindle and the drumsticks of fraud.

nature fights back
ross gelbspan

Katrina traumatized not only the residents of the Gulf Coast, but the rest of us as well. This was a fury we Americans have rarely experienced. The initial reactions following the storm recalled the typical scrambling of trauma victims: a frantic focus on other issues—any other issues—so people could avoid the central message. For days, the media was full of criticisms of the Federal Emergency Management Agency's (FEMA) slow reactions, the president's initial lack of urgency, and the failure of Louisiana authorities to provide proper evacuation planning. All this was a panicky effort to avoid confronting one of Katrina's underlying messages: the truly awesome power of inflamed nature.

The hurricane that struck the Gulf Coast in August 2005 started out naturally enough—as part of a traditional tropical storm cycle that generated a small, category 1 hurricane. However, after glancing off south Florida with winds of about 70 miles an hour, the storm was supercharged by the relatively blistering surface temperatures in the Gulf of Mexico (they were in the high 80s) and swelled to a megastorm, at one point reaching category 5 intensity, with winds of around 160 miles an hour. The National Weather Service named the storm Katrina. Its real name is global warming.

To be sure, countless extreme weather events have occurred over the past 10,000 years. But the increasing frequency and intensity of prolonged droughts, downpours, heat waves, and storms is indisputably a signature of the early stages of global warming. In the eight months before Katrina surfaced, for example, the world experienced a number of extreme events which are, by now, becoming almost commonplace.

- 2005 began with two feet of snow in the mountains around Los Angeles;[1]
- in January, a record 26.5 inches of snow fell on Boston in one weekend;[2]
- a rare ice storm in Georgia left 300,000 people without power;[3]
- 124–mph hurricane-force winds closed nuclear plants and left hundreds of thousands without power in Scandinavia and the United Kingdom;[4]
- in February, normally a dry period, intense rains killed 80 people and forced the evacuation of more than 40,000 people in Colombia and Venezuela;[5]
- a prolonged drought in the Midwest dropped water levels in the Missouri River to their lowest in recorded history;[6]
- a record-setting drought in Spain and Portugal triggered wildfires[7] and left water levels in France at their lowest in 30 years;[8]
- Mumbai received 37 inches of rain in one day;[9] and
- in Ethiopia, an unusually protracted drought left more than 1 million cattle herders facing serious water and food shortages.[10]

So, while Katrina's emergence was ultimately a natural event, her rapid acceleration to megastorm status bore distinctly human fingerprints. Like other planetary changes resulting from our relentless burning of coal and oil, Katrina is a harbinger of more radical and accelerated climate change.

what is global warming?

The unintended consequences of our burning of carbon fuels is altering the planet in unprecedented ways. For 10,000 years, to cite one example, we had about the same amount of heat-trapping carbon dioxide in the atmosphere—around 280 parts per million. But since the world began to industrialize in the 19th century and began to rely on coal and oil to power the process, that figure has jumped to 380—a level this planet hasn't seen for at least 650,000 years.[11] According to James Hansen of NASA, "There can no longer be genuine doubt that human-made gases are the dominant cause of observed [global] warming. This energy imbalance is the 'smoking gun' that we have been looking for."[12] By trapping heat that would otherwise have radiated back into space, human-generated carbon dioxide has thrown the planet's historical temperature equilibrium out of balance—with the earth becoming a net importer of heat. The rise in temperature has accelerated the planet's hydrological cycle. Sea levels have been rising twice as quickly over the past ten years as they were over the previous 100 years, according to recent measurements by NASA satellites.[13] That rise can be attributed in equal parts to the steady infusion of water from melting glaciers and ice caps and to the thermal expansion of the oceans themselves.[14] The consequences are terrifying.

Through most of history, nature has been portrayed as an ominous, arbitrary force whose threatening and unpredictable potential lurks constantly in the shadows of daily life. In today's insulated and electronic world, however, nature has generally come to be viewed as the passive context against which our more "real" activities are played out. I believe that as the trauma of Hurricane Katrina recedes, a different view of nature will surface in the general consciousness—through the inescapable recognition of our direct and active role in the making of Katrina.

irrefutable scientific evidence

Several recent studies put Katrina in the context of some larger changes we are seeing in the oceans.

A major study, led by Tim Barnett of the Scripps Institution of Oceanography, found that about 84 percent of the excess heat generated by human-induced global warming is being absorbed by the oceans. The researchers declared:

> A warming signal has penetrated into the world's oceans over the past 40 years. The signal is complex,

with a vertical structure that varies widely by ocean;
it cannot be explained by natural internal climate
variability or solar and volcanic forcing, but is well
simulated by two anthropogenically forced climate
models. We conclude that it is of human origin.[15]

Ocean warming is triggering a number of consequences—
the melting of ice caps, the acceleration of surface water
evaporation (manifest by the marked increase of intense, severe
downpours), the migration of marine species (blue mussels were
recently seen in the Arctic for the first time in at least 1,000
years[16]), as well as a change in tropical storm intensity.

Warmer ocean surface temperatures do not make more
tropical storms, but they do fuel them, making them more intense. An MIT study published about a month before Katrina
hit found that, since the mid–1940s when systematic record
keeping began, tropical storms all over the world have increased
in intensity and duration by about 50 percent in the past 30
years.[17] MIT researcher Kerry Emanuel noted that although
many of the fiercest storms of the past three decades haven't made
landfall when they were at peak intensity, "the near-doubling of
hurricanes' power during this period should be a matter of some
concern, as it's a measure of the (future) destructive potential
of these storms."[18] If climate change continues to warm both
seawater and the air above it for the rest of this century, as most
scientists expect, "future warming may lead to an upward trend
in tropical cyclone destructive potential, and—taking into account an increasing coastal population—a substantial increase in
hurricane-related losses in the 21st century,"[19] Emanuel warned.

Another study, one that was published just after Katrina
made landfall, found, that since the 1970s, there has been no
increase in the number of hurricanes, but there has been a big
increase in the proportion of those storms which reach categories 4 and 5.[20] Peter J. Webster of the Georgia Institute of
Technology, a principal author of the study, told the Associated
Press that "it's the warm water vapor from the oceans that drives
tropical storms, and as the water gets warmer the amount of
evaporation increases, providing more fuel for the tempests.

Between 1970 and 2004, the average sea surface temperature in the tropics rose nearly .5° Celsius."[21] For context, there is no record of that magnitude of temperature increase in any equivalent time period since reliable records began to be compiled (i.e., the last 150 years).

According to Webster's coauthor Judith Curry, also of Georgia Tech, the team is "confident that the measured increase in sea surface temperatures is associated with global warming, adding that the increase in category 4 and 5 storms 'certainly has an element that global warming is contributing to.'"[22] Kevin Trenberth, a noted expert in hurricane dynamics at the National Center for Atmospheric Research, wrote that

> trends in human-influenced environmental changes are now evident in hurricane regions. These changes are expected to affect hurricane intensity and rainfall, but the effect on hurricane numbers remains unclear. The key scientific question is not whether there is a trend in hurricane numbers and tracks—but rather how hurricanes are changing.[23]

Sir David King, Tony Blair's chief science adviser, was unequivocal about the connection:

> The increased intensity of hurricanes is associated with global warming ... We have known since 1987 the intensity of hurricanes is related to surface sea temperature and we know that, over the last 15 to 20 years, surface sea temperatures in these regions have increased by half a degree centigrade. So it is easy to conclude that the increased intensity of hurricanes is associated with global warming.[24]

Perhaps the most succinct summary came from the chairman of Britain's Royal Commission on Environmental Pollution, Sir John Lawton, who said of Katrina, "This *is* global warming."[25]

Nor did such reactions come only from scientists. A number of European political leaders spoke to connections between the current Bush administration's failure to address the climate crisis and the intensity of Katrina. One was British deputy prime minister John Prescott. Shortly after Katrina made landfall, he

linked America's refusal to tackle climate change to the devastation of the New Orleans hurricane, drawing a parallel between
the destroyed city and a number of small island states that are
being submerged by rising sea levels and have become extremely
vulnerable to hurricanes and strong sea surges. Prescott criticized
the US for failing to sign the Kyoto Protocol, an international
agreement on climate change that aims to slow global warming
by reducing emissions of greenhouse gases.[26]

usa: global warming is a hoax

While the massive destruction of Katrina left Americans in shock,
it should have been no surprise to the federal government. A
Katrina-like hit on New Orleans had been predicted for decades.
With even a modest degree of planning, its impact could have
been drastically minimized. For years, the US Army Corps of
Engineers has warned that New Orleans could not withstand
anything more than a relatively weak (category 3) hurricane.
Ten years ago, when an intense rainstorm killed six people in the
city, the Corps asked Congress to provide $430 million to shore
up levees and pumping stations. That money never materialized.

Which brings us to a larger failure of the Bush administration—one which is as apparent in the current chaos in Iraq
as it is in its failure in the Gulf Coast and in the larger area of
global warming: a chronic disregard for planning. Three years
ago, the New Orleans *Times-Picayune* reported that the corps
declared the Bush administration was spending less than 20
percent of what was needed to complete the fortification of
levees to protect the city. In the spring of 2001, FEMA cited a
hurricane strike on New Orleans as one of the three most likely
US disasters—along with a terrorist attack on New York City.
Nevertheless, by 2004, the Bush administration had cut funding
to the New Orleans district of the Army Corps of Engineers
by more than 80 percent, as Sidney Blumenthal reported recently in *Salon*. In 2004, Louisiana's congressional delegation
got Congress to appropriate about $60 million for flood protec-

tion for the city; the Bush administration reduced that figure to $10.4 million.

While the Bush administration cut funding to strengthen protective dikes and levees, Louisiana's congressional delegation was working to secure money for the restoration of wetlands along the state's coastline, to buffer the impact of storm surges. Louisiana officials estimated the cost of the project at about $14 billion. The delegation, however, was able to secure only a tiny fraction of that money—$570 million over four years, according to the *Times-Picayune*.

Whether the administration needed that money for its military pursuits in Iraq or for its reckless and unprecedented tax cuts is unclear, but it speaks volumes about the administration's insistence on denying the reality of global warming.

Regrettably, President Bush's antiplanning propensity flies in the face of physical changes overtaking the planet. When, several years ago, the Environmental Protection Agency (EPA) listed on its website the potential effects of climate change on the US, in a document known as "The National Assessment on Climate Change," the White House ordered the agency to remove all references to the dangers of global warming.[27] President Bush dismissed the meticulously researched document, which took four years to prepare and review, as a frivolous "product of bureaucracy."[28] In fact, the EPA document was based on the findings of more than 2,000 scientists from 100 countries reporting to the United Nations in what is the largest and most rigorously peer-reviewed scientific collaboration in history.

The findings of those scientists, working as part of the Intergovernmental Panel on Climate Change, gave rise, in 1997, to an international plan to try to allow our climate to stabilize. The plan, known as the Kyoto Protocol, was signed by President Clinton but was never ratified by the Senate. In its first iteration, the agreement called on the world's industrial nations to reduce their carbon emissions by 2012 to an average of 7 percent below 1990 levels.

One of George W. Bush's first acts as president was to withdraw the US from the Kyoto Protocol—not only because he seems ideologically antagonistic to the UN but also because of pressure from companies such as ExxonMobil and (coal producer) Peabody Energy, which stand to lose the most from cutbacks in the nation's fossil fuel use. As the president's chief climate negotiator, Harlan Watson, put it, "Kyoto would have hammered our economy and put millions of Americans out of work."[29]

The science has been unequivocal for more than a decade: to stabilize the climate, humanity must reduce its use of carbon fuels by 70 percent in a very short time.[30] And it has become overwhelmingly apparent that the pace of climate change is accelerating faster than scientists had anticipated even ten years ago.[31] In response to that finding, the Netherlands is already implementing a plan to reduce its emissions by 80 percent in 40 years. Tony Blair has committed Great Britain to a 60 percent reduction in 50 years. Germany has vowed to reduce emissions by 50 percent in 50 years. And, in 2005, French president Jacques Chirac called on the entire industrial world to cut emissions by 75 percent by the year 2050. The major industrial nations behind the agreement are virtually unanimous in their desire to dramatically accelerate the timetable for reducing emissions.

In contrast, the response of the Bush administration has been to take dead aim at the UN as the world's coordinating agency on climate change. Shortly after former deputy defense secretary Paul Wolfowitz was installed as director of the World Bank, he promptly promised massive investments in new coal technology.[32] (Coal has the heaviest carbon concentration of all fuels, making it the most potent contributor to global warming.) Following a year of secret negotiations, in 2005, President Bush announced a pact with Australia, the world's largest coal exporter, and several developing countries to develop "clean coal."[33] This purely voluntary agreement contradicts the binding goals of the Kyoto Protocol. It also ignores the physical fact that one cannot clean the carbon out of coal—it's the carbon that's being burned.

So no matter how much coal is "cleaned," it will continue to fuel the warming of the planet.

Additionally, Bush appointed John Bolton as US ambassador to the United Nations—a diplomat who has been consistently antagonistic to much of the work of the UN. Since a more aggressive UN-sponsored Kyoto Protocol—which has been signed or ratified by more than 180 nations—does not fit the president's agenda, his strategy boils down to sabotaging the authority of the United Nations in the area of climate change.

To the president, this sounds like a plan. To the rest of us, it seems like a shortcut to climate hell.

but why?

Very few people in America know that Katrina's real name is global warming, because the coal and oil industries have spent millions of dollars to keep the public in doubt about the issue. The reason is simple: to stabilize the climate, we must cut coal and oil use by 70 percent. That, of course, threatens the survival of one of the largest commercial enterprises in history.

In 1995, public utility hearings in Minnesota found that the coal industry had paid more than $1 million to four scientists who were public dissenters on global warming. ExxonMobil has spent more than $13 million since 1998 on an anti-global warming public relations and lobbying campaign. In 2000, Big Oil and Big Coal scored their biggest electoral victory yet when George W. Bush was elected president. That victory led to subsequent ones as he allowed the industry to dictate his climate and energy policies. For years, the fossil fuel industry has lobbied the media to accord the same weight to a handful of global warming skeptics that they do to the findings of the Intergovernmental Panel on Climate Change.

Against this background, the ignorance of the American public about global warming stands out as an indictment of the US media. When the press bothers to cover the subject of global warming, it focuses almost exclusively on the political and diplomatic aspects, not on what global warming is doing to our agriculture, water supplies, plant and animal life, public health, and weather. That President George H. W. Bush, during the 1992 election campaign, referred to Al Gore as "Ozone Man" and that a Republican-dominated Senate defeated a Clinton administration resolution to support Kyoto were accorded far more importance by a politically blindered press corps than the fact that the planet is moving toward runaway climate change.

Beyond the immediate political realm, moreover, I suspect Hurricane Katrina dealt a severe blow to the illusion among larger segments of the American public that we are somehow separate from and independent of nature. The word *natural* assumes a certain baseline set of conditions in our physical environment. For better or—more likely—for worse, those conditions have become moving targets because of our failure to break the stranglehold of big coal and big oil on our political process and move to a clean-energy economy. There is no part of the planet's internal dynamics that we are not affecting—through disruptive patterns of land use, through accelerating deforestation, and ultimately, through our burning of coal and oil. The emerging aspect of nature we would rather not acknowledge is neither passive nor predictable. Nature responds to our assaults in ways we cannot always anticipate. Underneath her fascination and beauty and delights and surprises, nature retains a terrible capacity for retribution.

Two years ago, in a new introduction to a reissued edition of his classic book *The End of Nature*, Bill McKibben wrote:

> The sadness that drove me to write this book in the first place has not really lifted…We didn't create this world, but we are busy decreating it…This buzzing, blooming, mysterious, cruel, lovely globe of mountain, sea, city, forest; of fish and wolf and bug and man of carbon and hydrogen and nitrogen—it has come unbalanced in our short moment on it. It's mostly us now.[34]

But nature isn't letting us off the hook as easily as Bill McKibben's lament suggests. She may lie dormant in the weeds, apparently oblivious to our insults. But just when we settle into the false security that we have mastered nature, she lets us know—with signals that are undeniable—that she keeps score, that the game progresses according to her timetable, not ours, and that she holds us accountable for our actions no matter how hard we try to deny them. As the late environmentalist and author of *Silent Spring* Rachel Carson tried so hard to tell us some 50 years ago: "Nature fights back."

Given that reality, the real question facing us all is this: Which in the long run is more dangerous? Stronger hurricanes or our own category 5 denial?

endnotes

1 Nick Madigan, "Soaked and Cloaked in the Wet White West," *New York Times*, January 4, 2005.

2 Donovan Slack, "Winter Whopper Buries Region, Snowfall, Wind Crush the Coast," *Boston Globe*, January 24, 2005.

3 Associated Press, "Georgia Getting Power Back After Ice Storm" *MSNBC*, January 31, 2005, http://www.msnbc.msn.com/id/6883882/.

4 *CNN.com*, "Three Dead as Gales Batter Britain," January 12, 2005, http://www.cnn.com/2005/WEATHER/01/12/britain.storm/index.html.

5 Reuters New Service, "Colombia, Venezuela Floods Death Toll Exceeds 80," *Epoch Times*, February 15, 2005, http://www.theepochtimes.com/news/5-2-15/26446.html.

6 Bob Mercer, "Drop in Big Muddy Roils Nation's Midsection, Long Drought Restricts Missouri River Region," *Boston Globe*, March 7, 2005.

7 David Evans, "Drought Tightens Its Deadly Grip in Europe," *RedOrbit*, July 18, 2005, http://www.redorbit.com/news/science/177847/drought_tightens_its_deadly_grip_in_europe/index.html.

8 David Evans, "France Rations Water as Drought Takes Hold," *Hindustan Times*, July 11, 2005, http://www.hindustantimes.com/news/181_1428085,0094.htm.

9 *BBCNews.com*, "Millions Suffer in Indian Monsoon," August 1, 2005, http://news.bbc.co.uk/2/hi/south_asia/4733897.stm.

10 Anthony Mitchell, "More Than a Million Face Extreme Food Shortages in Ethiopia," *Environmental News Network*, December 30, 2005, http://enn.com/today.html?id=9566.

11 Intergovernment Panel on Climate Change, *Third Assessment Report*, (Geneva Switzerland: Intergovernmental Panel on Climate Change, 2001); also Andrew C. Revkin, "Rise in Gases Unmatched by a History in Ancient Ice," *New York Times*, November 25, 2005.

12 James Hansen et al., "Earth's Energy Imbalance: Confirmation and Implications," *Science* 308, no. 5727 (2005): 1431–1435.

13 Robert S. Boyd, "Sea Levels Rise Fast: 1 Inch in 10 Years," *Seattle Times*, July 10, 2005.

14 Thermal expansion refers to the fact that as water heats, it expands.

15 Tim P. Barnett et al., "Penetration of Human-Induced Warming into the World's Oceans," *Science* 309, no. 5732 (2005): 284–287.

16 Amitabh Avasthi, "Warming Arctic Sees Return of Blue Mussels After 1,000 Years," *National Geographic News*, December 21, 2005, http://news.nationalgeographic.com/news/2005/12/1221_051221_mussels.html.

17 Miguel Bustillo, "Storm Turns Focus to Global Warming," *Los Angeles Times*, August 30, 2005.

18 Lee Bowman, "Tropical Storms More Intense, New Research Shows," *Scripps Howard News Service*, July 31, 2005, http://www.shns.com/shns/g_index2.cfm?action=detail&pk=STORM-INTENSITY-07-31-05.

19 Kerry Emanuel, "Increasing Destructiveness of Tropical Cyclones over the Past 30 Years," *Nature*, July 31, 2005, http://www.nature.com/nature/journal/v436/n7051/full/nature03906.html.

20 P. J. Webster et al., "Changes in Tropical Cyclone Number, Duration, and Intensity in a Warming Environment," *Science* 309, no. 5742 (2005): 1844–1846.

21 Schmid, Randolph, "Experts Say Global Warming is Causing Stronger Hurricanes," *USA Today*, http://www.usatoday.com/weather/climate/2005-09-15-globalwarming-hurricanes_x.htm.

22 Ibid.

23 Kevin Trenberth, "Uncertainty in Hurricanes and Global Warming," *Science* 308, no. 5729 (2005): 1753–1754.

24 Andrew Buncombe, "King: Global Warming May Be to Blame," *Independent* (London), August 31, 2005.

25 Michael McCarthy, "As Hurricane Rita Threatens Devastation, Scientist Blames Climate Change," *Independent* (London), September 23, 2005.

26 Juliette Jowit and Ned Temko, "Prescott Links Global Warming to Katrina," *Observer* (London), September 11, 2005.

27 Andrew C. Revkin and Katharine Q. Seelye "Report by the EPA Leaves Out Data on Climate Change," *New York Times*, June 19, 2003.

28 Ross Gelbspan, *Boiling Point* (New York: Basic Books, 2004), 42.

29 Steve Connor, "Forget Kyoto Deal for Another 10 years, Says Bush Adviser," *Independent* (London), May 14, 2002.

30 Intergovernmental Panel on Climate Change, *Second Assessment Synthesis Of Scientific: Technical Information Relevant To Interpreting Article 2 Of The UN Framework Convention On Climate Change* (Geneva Switzerland: Intergovernmental Panel on Climate Change, 1995).

31 "Clive Cookson "Scientists Warn of New Anthropocene Age" *Financial Times*, August 26, 2004; also Michael McCarthy, "Global Warming 'far faster than expected'," *Independent* (London), November 9, 2000.

32 World Bank, "Working Together to Beat the Heat," news release, July 19, 2005, http://web.worldbank.org/WBSITE/EXTERNAL/NEWS/ 0,,contentMDK:20588140~pagePK:642 57043~piPK:437376~theSitePK:4607,00.html.

33 Vijay Joshi, "US Initiative on Climate Met with Cautious Praise, Skepticism in Asia, Europe," July 29, 2005, http://www.enn.com/today.html?id=8370.

34 Bill McKibben, *The End of Nature*, 2nd ed. (New York: Anchor Books, 1999).

how we survived the flood
charmaine neville

I was in my house when everything first started. When the hurricane came, it blew all the left side of my house off, and the water was coming in my house in torrents.

I had my neighbor, an elderly man, and myself, in the house with our dogs and cats, and we were trying to stay out of the water. But the water was coming in too fast. So we ended up having to leave the house.

We left the house and we went up on the roof of a school. I took a crowbar and I burst the door on the roof of the school to help people on the roof.

Later on, we found a flat boat, and we went around the neighborhood getting people out of their houses and bringing them to the school.

We found all the food that we could and we cooked and we fed people. But then, things started getting really bad.

By the second day, the people that were there, that we were feeding and everything, had no more food and no water. We had nothing, and other people were coming in our neighborhood. We were watching the helicopters going across the bridge and airlifting other people out, but they would hover over us and tell us "Hi!" and that would be all. They wouldn't drop us any food or water, or anything.

Alligators were eating people. There was all kinds of stuff in the water. There were babies floating in the water.

We had to walk over hundreds of bodies of dead people. People who we tried to save from the hospices, from the hospitals and from the old-folks homes. I tried to get the police to help us, but I realized they were in the same straits we were. We rescued a lot of police officers from the fifth district police station in the flat boat. The guy who was in the boat, he rescued a lot of them and brought them to different places so they could be saved.

We understood that the police couldn't help us, but we couldn't understand why the National Guard and them couldn't help us, because we kept seeing them but they never would stop and help us.

Finally it got to be too much. I just took all of the people that I could. I had two old women with no legs in wheelchairs, that I rowed from down there in that nightmare to the French Quarter, and I went back and got more people.

There were groups of us, there were about 24 of us, and we kept going back and forth and rescuing whoever we could get and bringing them to the French Quarter because we heard that there were phones in the French Quarter, and that there wasn't any water. And they were right, there were phones, but we couldn't get through to anyone.

I found some police officers. I told them that a lot of us women had been raped down there by guys, not from the neighborhood where we were, they were helping us to save people. But other men, and they came and they started raping women and they started killing, and I don't know who these people were. I'm not gonna tell you I know, because I don't.

But what I want people to understand is that if we hadn't been left down there like the animals that they were treating us like, all of those things wouldn't have happened. People are trying to say that we stayed in that city because we wanted to be rioting and we wanted to do this and we didn't have resources to get out, we had no way to leave.

When they gave the evacuation order, if we could've left, we would have left.

There are still thousands and thousands of people trapped in their homes in the downtown area. When we finally did get into the Ninth Ward, and not just in my neighborhood, but in other neighborhoods in the Ninth Ward, there were a lot of people still trapped down there ... old people, young people, babies, pregnant women. I mean, nobody's helping them.

And I want people to realize that we did not stay in the city so we could steal and loot and commit crimes. A lot of those young men lost their minds because the helicopters would fly over us and they wouldn't stop. We would make SOS on the flashlights, we'd do everything, and it really did come to a point, where these young men were so frustrated that they did start shooting. They weren't trying to hit the helicopters, they figured maybe they weren't seeing. Maybe if they hear this gunfire they will stop then. But that didn't help us. Nothing like that helped us.

Finally, I got to Canal Street with all of my people I had saved from back there.

I don't want them arresting anybody else. I broke the window in an RTA bus. I never learned how to drive a bus in my life. I got in that bus. I loaded all of those people in wheelchairs and in everything else into that bus, and we drove and we drove and we drove and millions of people were trying to get me to help them to get on the bus, too.

to render ourselves visible: women of color organizing and hurricane katrina
alisa bierria, mayaba liebenthal, and incite! women of color against violence

And that visibility which makes us most vulnerable is that which also is the source of our greatest strength.

—Audre Lorde

Peace,

> *I'm crying as I write ... I found out about this two days ago: Charmaine Neville, like hundreds of other women, [was] raped during the week of the storm ... I just received a link about Charmaine's efforts to rescue and help those in her community survive the flood water in the Ninth Ward, while at the same time [being] sexually violated. There has to be some form of community accountability for the sexual and physical violence women and children endured. I'm not interested in developing any action plan to rebuild/organize a people's agenda in New Orleans without a gender analysis and a demand for community accountability.*

> *—Shana[1]*

Shana Griffin wrote this e-mail on September 15, 2005, almost three weeks after Hurricane Katrina nearly consumed the Gulf Coast. Writing to a community of organizers, Shana, a black woman and longtime New Orleans organizer herself, found herself having to render visible the experience of women of color in the context of disaster—both the disaster of the storm itself and the disaster of oppression in the context of the storm. The story of Hurricane Katrina and its aftermath is in many ways a story of a shifting boundary between the visibility and invisibility of people most impacted by these disasters, and the dangers and opportunities inherent in both.

Outsiders (one of the authors of this essay among them) were often riveted by the news coverage of the events after the actual storm, overwhelmed by image after image of unbearable suffering. Commentators recognized that the people left behind in New Orleans were predominantly poor and predominantly black. The brutal reality of US poverty—poverty that disproportionately embeds itself in the lives of black people, of southerners, and of women and children—was exposed on television screens. "We learned that one way to see people who were invisible before," Shana says, "is to leave them behind."

Oppressors render the oppressed invisible or hypervisible, relative to how the situation benefits their agenda. Invisibility can be used as a tool of oppression, because if a people can't be seen, then their work can be discounted, their experience of violence and oppression can go without recourse, and their lives can be devalued. Hypervisibility, on the other hand, can be used to stigmatize people or to easily identify them as an object of fear or a target for violence. Those New Orleanians who were left behind after the storm were, before the storm, rendered invisible as the class experiencing some of the most damaging consequences of the United States' relentlessly unjust economic system. Their post-Katrina hypervisibility, as represented by the media, also left them vulnerable to racist and sexist stereotyping. The manipulation of depictions of oppressed people within institutions such as the mainstream media is intentional—the representation of our bodies is made to signify their truths and the presence of our bodies is erased to conceal their secrets.

For example, during the week Katrina consumed the Gulf Coast, mainstream media attention quickly shifted from the vast institutional failure of the response by the local and federal governments to more salacious stories of violence, "looting," and "lawlessness" by a population that was mostly black. As a result, the media justified a practically nonexistent rescue operation by focusing on calls for more criminalization and population control rather than rescue. It was in this revised political context set by the media's focus that extensive reports of sexual violence began to publicly surface. Journalists rapidly reported numerous accounts of "unconfirmed sexual assaults."

Sexual violence usually happens behind the closed doors of our homes and institutions and is often rendered invisible in the media and in public discourse. For this reason, one might believe that whenever the news media focuses on sexual violence, it's a good thing. However, the same media haphazardly recounting stories of sexual assault was also portraying the black people who were left behind—desperate and without basic needs such as food, water, and shelter—as violent, criminal looters. In the context of the egregiously racist and classist criminalization of these survivors of the storm, we must ask ourselves, why the focus on sexual assault now? Was it really to provide accountable reporting of a violence that was surely happening in the context of so many disasters occurring in the post-Katrina world of New Orleans and other Gulf Coast communities? Or was it to lure outside viewers into buying more newspapers and watching more 24–hour news channels by offering them scandalizing tales that would satisfy their racist and sexist curiosities? Who benefited?

On the other hand, the response of many activists to these media accounts of sexual assaults was to shift the focus away from the problem of sexual violence within the population of survivors and back to the massive violence being perpetrated on people in New Orleans by the local police, the National Guard, and other law enforcement bodies. Instead of figuring out strategies to take people's experiences of sexual violence seriously, the strategy was to bring the media's attention back to the "real" problems of institutional poverty, police violence, and the failure of government response. Sexual violence (along with its victims and perpetrators) is, again, rendered invisible in the name of ending racism.

In her article "New Orleans and Women of Color: Connecting the Personal and Political," Janelle White, a feminist activist-scholar and member of INCITE! New Orleans before being displaced after the hurricane, makes it clear that sexual violence after Katrina was perpetrated both by officials of the state (such as the police, the National Guard, and the FBI) and by men and boys of the New Orleans community. Janelle writes

> This is the more difficult abuse to speak of, especially for women of color, as we have no desire to aid further in stereotyping, demonizing, and criminalizing men and boys of color, particularly men and boys of African descent. Nonetheless, it is a painful truth that must be spoken. The bottom line that this catastrophe painfully demonstrates is, yet again, how women and girls of color are at the intersection of violence perpetrated upon marginalized communities, both by external social forces and by those within our communities.[2]

Women of color had to figure out how to talk about sexual violence happening to women and children of color on their own terms, rather than on the terms of the media landing a sensationalized story that satisfies the racist fantasy of white America, or on the terms of those activists—including black men—who dismiss the stories of rape as distracting from the "real" problem of racism and classism. They had to create strategies to render themselves truly visible—not as representations of someone else's agenda, but as their authentic selves experiencing and resisting the full brunt of oppressions and disasters colliding into one another.

This is where Shana's letter comes in. Shana is a member of both the national collective and New Orleans chapter of INCITE! While participating in a coalition of organizations led by local people of color that was formed to develop a grassroots response to the injustices uncovered and made worse by Hurricane Katrina, she realized that a radical gender analysis was missing in their work. Further, she recognized that the racist and sexist legal system that was brutalizing people left behind in New Orleans, including women of color, and the institutions we are told to go to for support when we are raped or abused were one and the same. When she spoke in the coalition about the urgent need to integrate a gender justice agenda that recognized how sexual and domestic violence was facilitated by the storm, she was accused of being "divisive."

Finally, after hearing about Charmaine Neville's horrifying experience, women of color in New Orleans asserted their own political agency by demanding that women of color be *seen*. For the experience of women of color to be rendered visible, we would need to acknowledge that the experiences of violence within communities and violence perpetrated onto communities by the state intersect primarily on the bodies of women of color. Recognizing that pathways such as the criminal justice system and the medical industry were not available because of the devastation caused by the hurricane and because of the violence these institutions were themselves perpetrating, women of color organizers also demanded a *community accountability* response to violence against women and children. By calling for a system of accountability within the community, women of color opened up an opportunity for communities to assert their own political agency by developing responses to intracommunity violence, while also organizing against violence perpetrated on the community by the state. Members of INCITE! New Orleans continue to affirm that the problem of rape *is* a real problem that deserves and demands as much of a politicized and powerful response as workers' rights or environmental justice. As Shana explains:

> To me, it's not enough to have a solid race and class analysis, because beyond those two, you also need a gender analysis. Because of the absence of the gender analysis of many agencies, organizations who identify as women of color organizations have to constantly fight to render ourselves visible and at the same time, we have to justify our existence in the work that we're trying to do.[4]

invisibility and organizing strategies

Domestic and sexual violence is facilitated by other disasters. Women of color bear the brunt of compromised safety during a disaster and after. Shortly after Katrina, a visiting representative of Florida's disaster management team told New Orleans' mayor Ray Nagin's Bring New Orleans Back Commission that domestic violence will increase. There's little doubt why. Cramped living conditions (with families housed in small travel trailers or in overcrowded homes and shelters) and high stress situations increase the prevalence of domestic violence.[5] The lack of affordable housing in New Orleans, which contributes to domestic and sexual violence, will not improve for low-income people anytime soon due to the decision of federal housing officials to raze 5,000 public housing units in an effort to drive poor people permanently out of the city.[6] With the breakdown of communities and the loss of old neighbors—and the loss of just about all neighbors—because of widespread displacement and destruction of affordable housing, community accountability for rape and abuse becomes even harder to implement. Building and reconnecting communities must become a critical and central antiviolence strategy, now more than ever.

Despite the correlation between the housing crisis and sexual and domestic violence, there are few emergency shelters in the city (none of which are readily accessible and available), and no battered women's shelters. However, the lack of battered women's shelters and the destruction of institutional systems designed to support domestic violence has actually revealed some weaknesses of this system that existed before the hurricane. A New Orleans-based coalition of domestic violence service providers working to support women after the storm have found themselves assisting women in a variety of circumstances, not just as domestic violence survivors. The providers have come to realize since the storm that they must support survivors of domestic violence in the context of many kinds of violence—including extreme poverty, stranger harassment, the loss of their children, criminalization, poor health care, etcetera—not just as it relates to their experience of being in an abusive relationship. But all of these problems existed before the storm, especially for the most marginalized survivors of domestic violence. The context may have looked different, but the fact that domestic violence exists in a context of so many other kinds of violence and oppressions is not a new phenomenon. In fact, radical women of color have recognized that "violences" against women are not isolated from one another, and we women of color have been recommending that the anti-domestic violence movement take a broader, more integrated approach to supporting women from the beginning. However, this recommendation has, in the past, fallen on deaf ears in order for the problem of domestic violence to be taken seriously by the people with the most power (who, incidentally, are also people who do not want to discuss issues such as poverty and criminalization) instead of the most marginalized people. Why did it take the flooding of a city for this point to finally be legitimate?

The marginalization and invisibility of the analysis and political strategies of women of color has weakened the potential response of anti-domestic violence services to support survivors before and after the hurricane. Nationally, policy makers and government funders prioritize battered women's shelters over longer-term strategies, often recommended by radical women of color, such as community organizing and community-based accountability. However, after a disaster like this one, when shelters are destroyed through floods, and when there are no crisis lines to call, and when the police are perpetrating sexual violence themselves, we see that these longer-term strategies are urgently needed now. Community organizing and communi-ty-based accountability are the things we have left when the systems have collapsed. Further, these strategies often integrate a plan to address the institutional conditions that fortify do-mestic violence.

Mainstream antiviolence organizations identify battered women's shelters and other crisis services as "meat and potatoes" services, since those services receive the lion's share of private and public funding, while community organizing, if considered at all, is relegated to a secondary role. If the antiviolence movement had "centered" the experiences and antiviolence strategies of women of color over the past 30 years, pouring its resources into community organizing and mobilization, the capacity of women to respond to violence in the context of natural disaster would be radically different. Mainstream antiviolence organizations would have known that women cannot depend on police, but that we must depend on each other to develop strategies to stay safe. We all would have stronger community connections and more resilient community-based resources to help support and protect each other. In terms of Katrina, that might have taken the form of collectively securing rides out of the city before the worst of the storm arrived, or rescuing each other from attics and rooftops, or making a plan to ensure that the local child abuser is watched and prevented from hurting people while we are escaping. Further, when community members were able to organize plans to help evacuate and rescue their neighbors, they might have been able to anticipate the undermining and thwarting of their efforts by government agencies, such as that which occurred in New Orleans after Katrina. Radical women of color strategies for ending violence open up opportunities not just for ending sexual and domestic violence, but for nurturing more organized communities in which people are better able to take care of one another in the face of all kinds of disasters.

whitening new orleans

Perhaps one of the more insidious effects of invisibility is that mainstream populations and government agencies will not acknowledge that you are gone. Hypervisibilty and misrepresentation, on the other hand, will ensure you do not come back. For example, in a meeting about the shortage of public housing in New Orleans, city council member Oliver Thomas said that "we don't need soap opera watchers all day."[7] Also, Representative Richard H. Baker, a Republican from Baton Rouge, was overheard telling lobbyists that "we finally cleaned up public housing in New Orleans. We couldn't do it, but God did."[8] Thomas's and Baker's statements invoke intensely hateful stereotypes about former public housing residents—a group that is disproportionately composed of low-income black women and children. These are the people, apparently, that Thomas, Baker, and others do not want to come back, and comments such as these essentially justify the permanent displacement of thousands of public housing residents.

Population control policies, such as the destruction of affordable housing, denial of health care, lack of environmentally safe public schools, and lack of other critical community services, intentionally block particular people—especially poor women of color—from returning home. These policies create a *forced* migration and displacement of people of African descent and other people of color from New Orleans. They de facto change the demographic nature of a city renowned for its African traditions and rich multicultural legacy, radically transforming and whitening New Orleans. Furthermore, Avis Jones-DeWeever of the Institute for Women's Policy Research notes that "more women than men left the region after the storm" and that low-income women of color in particular are having a difficult time coming back home.[9] The institute has found that before Katrina, women made up 56 percent of the local workforce, but only 46 percent today; the number of families headed by single mothers in the metropolitan area has dropped from 51,000 to less than 17,000; and food stamp usage by those single mothers who have returned has quadrupled.[10]

Unfortunately, white progressive and radical Left volunteers that have come to "rebuild" in the name of altruism and charity also contribute to the changing demographics of the city. Though hundreds of nonprofits, NGOs, university urban planning departments, and foundations have come through the city, they have paid little attention to the organizing led by people of color that existed before Katrina and that is struggling now more than ever. A look at who and what gets funding in New Orleans, from foundations to support work, reveals the priorities of these foundations and the entire nonprofit system. Organizations that represent their work through quick and quantifiable accomplishments are rewarded by the system. Foundations are not only drawn to them but are pressured by their own donors to fund them.

Alternative ways of organizing that are not hastily put together, that are thoughtful, that take the time to develop strategies for community investment and accountability, and ensure that marginalized communities are centered in the process are not as attractive to funders, even though these strategies have more staying power in the long run and more potential for long-term transformation. The ways in which foundations fund progressive work are often counterproductive to revolutionary movement building and also tend to specifically marginalize radical women of color organizing strategies over more familiar white-dominated strategies.

These racist and paternalistic attitudes are not just embodied in foundations but in many nonlocal volunteers as well. Organizations predominantly consisting of white folks who are not from the area have brought in thousands of white volunteers to help with the rebuilding of New Orleans. Some of these groups may have one or two people of color in leadership, but the majority of the leadership are white. Although some of their relief work has been productive, there has not been consistent collaboration or solidarity with local-based organizing—much of it led by women of color—that has existed and continues to exist in New Orleans.[11] One group's posters paternalistically state, "Restoring Hope and Teaching Civic Responsibility," as if the people of New Orleans (which was majority people of color before the storm) need white folks to do either. "Restoring hope," in particular, calls to mind a colonial/missionary value system in which the largely white volunteers have a mission to spread hope and opportunities to the native New Orleanians. "Teaching civic responsibility" to local folks also falls in line with a pseudo-colonial agenda of instructing the "backward" locals in how to behave as a civilized citizenry. Or perhaps the idea is to "teach civic responsibility" to white volunteers on the backs of people of color, which also objectifies survivors of the disaster, who may not want their lives to be a training ground for well-meaning white people. On the same poster, the artwork predominantly features black women, giving viewers the impression that the group is predominantly led by black women—it isn't. While this particular poster illustrates several tensions in the relationship between nonlocal white volunteers and the locals they seek to "help," many organizations (including faith-based groups, relief-based groups, and radical left organizations) have problematic, uncritical positions on the impact of mass white volunteerism in New Orleans. White-dominated organizations' failure to use their significant resources to support local people of color organizing exemplifies the process of rendering invisible the rich legacy of social justice organizing in New Orleans, while at the same time they consciously use images of black women and other people of color to legitimize themselves to funders and to local communities of color.

Furthermore, the white volunteers coming to New Orleans benefit from their experience, but they remain unaccountable to local folks. Many nonlocal people in the city are here to "get experience" working in a disaster zone. These character-building experiences in some cases actually have the capacity to compromise women's and other community members' safety, many of whom have lost everything. For example, white volunteers participated in the first wave of intensified post-Katrina gentrification; organizations created cramped conditions for hundreds of volunteers, which helped to increase sexual assault; and activists organized planning processes that planned local people right out of the process. Essentially, when people treat you like you don't matter, you don't feel safe. Many of these volunteers are coming from a contemporary form of activist tourism—in which a US or European radical activist tours "hot spots" for revolutionary work around the world to increase her activist cred. This kind of "solidarity" activity objectifies people of color—again, our bodies are used to signify their truths. The viewer is the white activist, the viewed is the oppressed person of color; the encounter between the two is unidirectional—objectifier and objectified.

An alternative way of considering solidarity was put forward in a recent article, "Rethinking Solidarity," by the Refugio Collective of Brooklyn, New York. They write, "It's the unaltered position of power and privilege that much of this [US-based] activism is rested upon...But accountability is a *process*, one that moves in both directions and requires more thoughtful reflection of our position in this country in relation to others."[12] Volunteers in New Orleans who are outsiders, especially those who are white, need to engage in humble and thoughtful reflection about how one should take up space in a devastated community that is undergoing fast-tracked, ruthless gentrification. Otherwise, the whitening of New Orleans will continue and will instigate more violence, such as that which results when white volunteers call the police into neighborhoods that are already terrorized by law enforcement violence. Further, due to discrimination, volunteers who decide to stay and get paid work are given preferential treatment over New Orleanians of color that were there before. The volunteers can often afford skyrocketing rents in neighborhoods they would not have dared to enter before the storm. This is called back-door disaster gentrification (also known as volunteer fallout). Nonlocal allies could do work in solidarity with New Orleans from where they live by supporting displaced survivors in their own local communities, but those who choose to work in New Orleans often do so because they are drawn by the excitement of realizing their own political ambitions (whether they be pursuing pet projects in devastated neighborhoods or simply adding this town to their activist résumés). As the Refugio Collective writes, "So long as social movements remain something to go and see as opposed to something we live, then despite our best intentions, we find ourselves only taking up space and inserting ourselves in communities in a way that reflects our internalized colonial attitudes and privileges."[13]

authentic visibility

The authentic visibility of the oppressed, in this case, women of color, is sometimes perceived by the Left as an actual threat to solidarity instead of an opportunity for richer, more effective, and more relevant political strategies. However, when the experiences, ideas, and lives of women of color are centered, instead of being considered "divisive" or "secondary," a politics emerges that has the possibility of making the entire movement better for everyone. When women of color assert an authentic existence and visibility that acknowledge the intersections of oppressions within the public and private spheres, we create opportunities for everyone to construct new ways to think about organizing for justice and liberation. As Andy Smith, a founding member of the INCITE! national collective, puts it, radical women of color organizing is not just about *including* women of color in organizing agendas, it's about *re-centering* women of color in organizing agendas, allowing their authentic experiences to guide our ways of thinking about justice. Andy writes in her article "Re-Centering Feminism" that "radical women of color organizing is not simply based on a narrow politics of identity but more on a set of political practices designed to eliminate the interlocking systems of oppression based on heteropatriarchy, white supremacy, capitalism and colonialism, a vision that is libratory for all peoples."[14]

If we were to re-center women of color in the work of organizing in the context of Hurricane Katrina, we would recognize that sexual violence is a serious political issue, both as it relates to community violence and safety in notoriously unsafe spaces such as the Superdome and as it relates to the military occupation that took place in the name of "restoring order" to New Orleans. We would realize how critical it is to develop our own community-based resources and responses to violence within our communities, as well as to violence targeting our communities, such as police violence and environmental racism. Centering the lives of women of color—because they are often the primary caregivers for both children and elders—might have helped us anticipate the way that children would be targeted in chaos and the way in which people with disabilities and elders might be trapped in nursing homes and hospitals. Centering undocumented immigrant women, recognizing that often when they experience domestic or sexual violence they do not call the police for fear of deportation, we might have anticipated the dangers faced by undocumented people during and after the hurricane—in which they risked deportation if they asked for help and risked drowning if they didn't.

Further, instead of demanding that foundations "include" women of color projects among their funding priorities and value women of color organizing styles in their assessments, we may recognize that depending on volatile foundation-based funding—often based on "flavor of the month" priorities—is not a sustainable practice for long-term revolutionary projects. By re-centering the experiences of women of color, we may realize that we need alternative strategies to fund our grassroots movement-building work.

Though we welcome genuine solidarity, women of color will not wait for men and white people to figure out the rich opportunities that exist in their potential solidarity with us. Radical women of color organizing is about manifesting our own political agency and forging our own authentic visibility as we work for the liberation for all people. The New Orleans chapter of INCITE! is a collective of local women of color that is building powerful mechanisms for facilitating women's access to safety and health care as it builds a political base for revolutionary change. The collective is developing the Women's Health and Justice Initiative, an exciting multidimensional collaborative organizing project to improve women of color's access to quality, affordable, and safe health care services. The initiative's projects—including the establishment of a women's health clinic—will be used as fertile ground for organizing women of color who experience violence, exploitation, and discrimination—particularly those women who are poor, immigrant, queer, homeless, heads of households, disabled, sex workers, incarcerated or formerly incarcerated, young, and public housing residents. The initiative integrates a consciousness of the impact that violence against women, poverty, gender inequalities, toxic communities, trauma, and coercive sterilization policies have on women's health. Providing services is not enough to ensure that women and girls of color have accurate and adequate information to make healthy decisions about their bodies, their sexuality, and reproduction. Therefore, their strategy incorporates both health services to meet women's immediate needs and community organizing for gender, racial, economic, and environmental justice.

INCITE! New Orleans is also building a Women of Color Resource and Organizing Center, which will serve as a hub for women of color organizing in the city. The center will include a radical women of color lending library, meeting space, a cluster of ten computers for community access, and a comfortable environment for women to hang out. The center will also provide a host of programs and activities organized and run by local women and girls of color to end violence against women of color and the community they live in.

INCITE! New Orleans' organizing method takes an intersectionality approach that includes an analysis of gender, race, class, citizenship status, sexuality, and a critique of privilege. They try to organize from an unfragmented approach, meaning they don't expect people to walk through the door and drop three-fourths of themselves and come in as just a woman or just a black person."[15] When asked how this analysis informs the politics of a health clinic for women of color, Shana explained:

> [T]he purpose of the clinic is to improve low-income and uninsured women of color's health care access and to promote a holistic and community-centered approach to primary health care. At the same time we look at the oppression and violence that have impact on the health status of women and to improve those situations. It's more than providing health care services; it's also about challenging the conditions that limit our access and our opportunities, such as

poverty, racism, gender-based violence, imperialism, and war. We see it as more than just a clinic—we want it to also be an organizing center that can meet immediate needs while also working for racial, gender, economic, and environmental justice.[16]

Volunteers from all over the country, mostly women of color, have come to New Orleans to support INCITE! New Orleans' work. Through relationship building, following the leadership of local women of color, and learning about the political and cultural context of New Orleans, INCITE! New Orleans has been able to develop an alternative volunteer model that is conscious of the dangers of "activist tourism" and works to not operate within a colonial framework. Volunteers agree to stay for a limited period of time. They engage in support work that increases the capacity of local women of color organizing. And when they return home, they work to support Katrina survivors in their local areas, either to help them safely return to the Gulf Coast or get settled in their new location.

Women of color engage in this work for safety, visibility, and general health and well-being because it is still a reality that when organizing in larger circles, women of color often have to push to be heard. All too often, we haven't been heard, our experiences haven't been considered, and others put together organizing plans, campaigns, mobilizations, and projects without us. Ultimately, being seen is about creating our own meaning for ourselves, on our own terms, and then using the lessons from our lives to create plans for justice.

---

endnotes

1   Shana Griffin, e-mail message to dozens of local activists and organizers mobilizing after Katrina, September 15, 2005.
2   Janelle L. White, "New Orleans and Women of Color: Connecting the Personal and Political," *Satya*, November 2005.
3   INCITE! Women of Color Against Violence is a national activist organization of feminists of color advancing movement to end violence against women of color and their communities through direct action, critical dialogue, and grassroots organizing.

4   Elena Everett, "Confronting Gender after Katrina: An Interview with Shana Griffin," *Dissident Voice*, August 25, 2006.

5   Suzanne Batchelor, "Assault Risk Rises in Jammed Post-Katrina Homes," *Women's ENews*, June 22, 2006, http://www.feminist.com/news/vaw67.html.

6   Susan Saulny, "5,000 Public Housing Units in New Orleans Are To Be Razed," *New York Times*, June 15, 2006.

7   Martin Savidge, "Some on City Council Want Housing Reserved for Those Willing to Work," *NBC Nightly News*, February 21, 2006, http://www.msnbc.msn.com/id/11485681/.

8   Charles Babington, "Some GOP Legislators Hit Jarring Notes in Addressing Katrina," *Washington Post*, September 10, 2005.

9   Frank Donze, "Plight of women in N.O. Decried: Single Moms Dwindle in City, Study Shows," *Times-Picayune*, August 19, 2006.

10 Eric Williams, Olga Sorokina, Avis Jones-DeWeever, and Heidi Hartmann, *The Women of New Orleans and the Gulf Coast: Multiple Disadvantages and Key Assets for Recovery, Part II. Gender, Race, and Class in the Labor Market*, (Washington, DC: Institute for Women's Policy Research, 2006).

11 Just a few examples of women of color led organizing projects in New Orleans include INCITE! New Orleans, Families and Friends of Louisiana's Incarcerated Children, the Women's Health and Justice Initiative, the Institute for Women and Ethnic Studies, and the Ashe Cultural Center.

12 Refugio Collective (Adjoa Jones de Almeida, Dana Kaplan, Paula X. Rojas, Eric Tang, and M. Mayuran Tiruchelvam), "Rethinking Solidarity," *Left Turn*, May–June 2006.

13 Refugio Collective, "Rethinking Solidarity."

14 Andrea Smith, "Re-Centering Feminism," *Left Turn*, May–June 2006.

15 Everett, "Confronting Gender."

16 Everett, "Confronting Gender."

wade in the water
tiffany brown

The waters have receded, but the city, the region, is still drown-ing. At first it was the waters from the storm; now it is the waters of inequality. For scores of people left abandoned in waist-high water, on rooftops and bridges, the dividing line for poor, disenfranchised people became blaringly clear. It became clear for those of us who believed that the civil rights movement of the 1950s and 1960s had changed hearts and minds along with laws. It became clear for those of us who bought into the American dream of "pulling yourself up by your bootstraps" and the African proverb "it takes a village..." because the bootstraps washed away in the floodwaters and the village watched on tele-vision sets across the nation as the battle ensued over what termi-nology to use to describe those who were stranded. Meanwhile, our world leader vacationed at home and his mother would later say while visiting the Astrodome in Houston, "Everybody is so overwhelmed by the hospitality. And so many of the people in the arena here, you know, were underprivileged anyway so this is working very well for them," implying that their new lives—on a cot in a makeshift shelter, not knowing what happened to their homes, their family, their neighbors—were even better than their lives before the storm.

The line dividing the poor from the rich became crystal clear. The reality ended up on the front pages of newspapers delivered at the door and on television sets in the homes of those who thought "that kind of thing" only happens some-where else. Those who were left in a ravaged land now have a recent example to illustrate what they've known all along: being poor and colored sucks. "Wade in the water," the words of an old Negro spiritual, has had a resurgence and has new meaning. But God didn't trouble these waters. These waters have begun to smell with the bodies of the forgotten. These waters are still murky with governmental ineptitude. The waters we wade are filled with both bounty and torture: The bounty of the human spirit and kindness that has flowed abundantly among and toward people displaced around the country, from their neighbors new and old. The torture of the loss of the safety and familiarity of home and the disappearance of huge sections of culture; the torture of fear, the fear of the unknown, as thousands start anew in a strange land with a new reality and a few old reminders about race and class; the torture of how quickly we forget the threats that exist in the water even as it recedes.

There was a time when the water from hoses punished the bodies of men, women, and children standing up for what they believed in, and the news came and shamed the nation into action. Now the news comes and governmental onlookers have counterprogramming to tell you that what you have just witnessed was just a figment of your imagination or liberal bias. We are supposed to believe that conservative bias does not exist when we see footage of survivors with reporting that describes some as "looking for food" and others as "looting," depending on the racial identity of the person in the clip.

Despite the lack of government response, not every Katrina story is one of gloom. Some whose lives were altered by the storm have started anew and have their own adventure to tell. They are living well, being grateful for what they do have, and trying something new. Others are living a new life that is not the one that they dreamed of, but it's the one they have as they wait for normalcy to return. Still others struggle to maintain hope. Hope and faith were two things many marchers learned about in the civil rights movement of long ago. They have been called upon today, in the wake of the storm, by many who were not around then. This hope is fostered by the outpouring of support by the countless number of people who saw the reports and opened their homes and hearts to those in need. This hope is fostered by the many New Orleanians who were the heroes during the storm, whether they were "looting" food from a hotel and cooking it for the masses of people trapped in a drowning city, as one resident did, or hotwiring a bus and making several trips to get people out of harm's way, as another resident did. This hope is fostered by the countless workers who stayed in the hospitals to care for the sick or left their supplies to help the neighboring hospital until it too could be evacuated.

Not all the stories are spirit killing. But many are. One of my friends went to New Orleans six months after the eye of Katrina landed—he was taking part in a 144-mile protest march from Mobile, Alabama to New Orleans. My friend said that when the march reached New Orleans, veterans of the Iraq war who were marching with him were overcome by the waves of memory triggered by the devastation and began to exhibit telltale symptoms of post-traumatic stress disorder—flashbacks, irritability, insomnia—just from the sight of the destruction.

Having lived in the Gulf region from Mobile to Houston for most of my life, with most of my time spent in New Orleans, I was largely unfazed by the physical destruction of the area. Some of the buildings I knew so well exist now only as memories. Never mind the loss of physical structures. For me, it is the loss of what's really irreplaceable that rips at my core. It is the loss of stories that span generations. It is the loss of life, culture, photos, dolls, evidence of better days.

In talking about Hurricane Katrina, I focus on New Orleans because that is where I am from. It is an obvious place to start since the devastation there has affected the economy of an entire state. It is an obvious place to start because it was where the largest concentration of people who were abandoned lived. When people think New Orleans, they think jazz, Mardi Gras, and gumbo; they think Black Indians, Creoles, above-ground cemeteries, and voodoo; they think "*laissez les bon temps roulez*"— let the good times roll. Yet in that same place, there were countless unemployed and close to 30 percent of the population lived below the poverty level. But none of that matches the images on the news. None of that matches the streets I once called home, where my friends and I took the streetcar to go to school. New Orleans has become unrecognizable, not just the streets, but the people. Their eyes have changed and certainly their view.

Every time I recall August 29, 2005, it is like remembering a bad dream. Like many from New Orleans, I'd thought, it won't be that bad—I'd heard the stories of hurricanes Betsy and Camille. I'd been ordered to evacuate before and the hurricane would always turn and not make landfall at all. How could this be any different? But it was. The hurricane destroyed people's homes, their world. It destroyed any myth we might have held about a national conscience, an all-encompassing spirit of compassion: compare the national response to the victims of the hurricane and the response to the victims of the Asian Tsunami of 2004 or the September 11, 2001 attacks.

I am honestly tired of recounting my feelings about Katrina. I want to get back to a sense of normalcy. But what is normal or routine when too much time has passed since the storm hit, and every day people I know and love still fight with insurance companies and filter through what is fact or rumor about what they'll get, about the damage that has occurred? I am tired of talking about how race does matter with people who already know or with those whose minds I will never change. I am tired of hearing folks say the evacuees are better off than they were before the storm—I am left wondering how being homeless, jobless, often not surrounded by the familiarity of family, friends, your community is better off; or how an entire people can be accused for the increase in crime and murder in their transplanted homes. I am tired of feeling hopeless and useless in the face of the daunting task of rebuilding a community. I am tired of hearing the deafening silence about the current health crisis faced by the people who survived the storm, the poor who walked through waters filled with toxins from Cancer Alley that could potentially change future generations, gifting them with birth defects, with chronic illnesses, with premature death. I am tired of hearing even the stories of rebuilding when no one talks about the question of rebuilding for whom? I am tired of hearing the stories of rebuilding when the faces of those we saw penned in the Superdome or cordoned off on bridges, of those somehow "better off," are not included in any of the conversations; the voices that simply asked for water and food are still being ignored.

Most of all, I am tired of waiting for the mass outrage to occur. Not the outrage that is voiced in polite and not-so-polite conversation among ourselves, but the kind that spurs action. Weeks after the storm, Kanye West, a Grammy award-winning producer and hip-hop artist, said on national television at a charity event, "George Bush doesn't care about black people." Certainly, that was a call to arms. I thought the revolution would actually be televised, at least by the hip-hop generation. I thought that the leaders of yore would have their own resurgence and take up the campaign that was happening when Dr. Martin Luther King, Jr. died. Shouldn't this qualify as a Poor People's Campaign? Hasn't the event of the hurricane, storm surge, and the fate of the forgotten and stranded highlighted the plight of the poor? Hasn't it highlighted the underlying racism and classism that exist in this country? Where are the individuals asking questions about who is getting the rebuilding jobs? Where are the individuals asking questions about what happened to the millions of dollars collected in the name of Katrina survivors by various charitable organizations? Where is the outrage that spurs us as a nation into action? Or does the hue of the people just allow us to sit by and say, "not now"? I think that sounds reminiscent of other moments in our history.

Tired or not, my exhaustion will not make the issue go away. So instead of talking about the effects of Katrina in its most obvious forms, I want to address the fact that New Orleans prepared for an election shortly after the storm, one in which our government, the beacon of democracy, disenfranchised thousands. Thousands were denied their right to vote. Could it be remnants of a Jim Crow South? The high-tech devices used by Iraqi citizens living in the United States to vote in an election in a war-torn nation an ocean away were somehow not available to allow displaced voters from the Gulf Coast region a chance to vote in an election only a few states away. I want to deal with the fact that the United Nations met and made a commitment to end world poverty in 2000; it is 2006 and little or no progress has been made—including here in the United States. I want to hear about what we're going to do about the fact that long after the waters have receded and the victims are supposedly safe, some of the poor are still alive but we're not well, here in this country and abroad.

I found, on reflecting on the events of the past year, like many others, that I still have unanswered questions that swirl in my head. Questions about next steps, about how to prevent something like this from happening again, and a host of others. But the only thing I know for sure is that Hurricane Katrina, along with all the events that followed, changed me. It has renewed my sense of purpose and has challenged me to do and be more. As it has with countless others, it has taught me about the resiliency of the human spirit. It has made some of the material things a little less important and the moments surrounding them a little more precious. It has reminded me about the value of friendship and family.

southerners on new ground: our lesbian, gay, bisexual, and transgender community
mandy carter

My name is Mandy Carter, and I live in Durham, North Carolina. I self-identify as a 58-year-old out southern black lesbian social justice activist whose roots in social justice organizing date back to 1968, when I participated in the Poor People's Campaign in Washington, DC.

I am one of the six cofounders of a group called Southerners On New Ground (SONG), based in Durham. SONG was founded in 1993 by a group of black and white southern lesbians. Its mission is to contribute to progressive movement across the South by developing and implementing transformative models of organizing that connect race, class, culture, gender, and sexual orientation and identity. Specifically, SONG integrates work against homophobia into freedom struggles in the South.[1]

A number of our members, supporters, and allies were in the Gulf Coast area hit by Hurricane Katrina on August 29, 2005. Like everyone else, we at SONG watched the storm and its aftermath in disbelief and horror. One of the questions that SONG folks asked each other repeatedly is why couldn't the federal government get relief supplies in to the thousands left stranded in New Orleans, especially to those at the New Orleans Superdome. I watched with tears streaming down my face as I saw image after image of predominantly black folk—especially the very old and the very young—sweltering in the heat, and then as I later saw subsequent television images of those who died from the sweltering heat.

I asked myself how it is that we can be the richest country in the world and we can't get help into New Orleans and the other Gulf Coast communities affected by Katrina. We then heard reports that many of the National Guard units that would have normally been called up in this situation were not available because they were stationed in Iraq. Adding insult to injury, how is it that the government can deploy US troops all the way across the world within days, yet can't get them down into Louisiana, Mississippi, and Alabama?

We were making phone calls and sending e-mails to all of our SONG contacts in the affected states. Meanwhile, calls were coming into our SONG office asking what we knew. SONG's initial response was to find out how grassroots, low-income, people of color, and LGBT folks were doing; what they needed; and how we could help. We found out that the most immediate need was for direct financial support to New Orleans and Gulf Coast community-based groups. SONG helped spread this news through our networks. SONG also joined the southern-wide effort to coordinate volunteers.

SONG's efforts were, in large part, informed by the People's Hurricane Relief Fund and Reconstruction Oversight Committee (PHRF). PHRF was founded on September 10, 2005, when more than 42 organizations convened in Baton Rogue, Louisiana, to lay groundwork for a coordinated network of community leaders and organizations with the capacity and organizational infrastructure to help meet the needs of Gulf Coast people devastated by Katrina's impact. PHRF wanted to facilitate an organizing process that would demand the participation of local, grassroots black and progressive leadership in the relief, return, and reconstruction process in New Orleans.[2] Further, the committee advocated financial support for direct "people-to-people," grassroots, community-based relief efforts led by the groups that were already working for poor people, people of color, environmental justice, racial justice, low-income housing, LGBT rights, and against domestic violence, to name a few.[3]

lgbt communities line up to help in the south

National, regional, state, and local lesbian, gay, bisexual, and transgender organizations lined up to lend aid in any way they could—an unprecedented joint effort disaster response by the LGBT community. For example, the San Francisco-based Rainbow World Fund partnered with America's Second Harvest, the country's largest food bank network, to transport food to survivors and secure additional warehouse space to assist food banks.

Several AIDS organizations warned that people in the disaster zone living with HIV/AIDS were at risk of serious illness caused by interruptions to their medical treatments as well as by exposure to water-borne pathogens. The National Association of People with AIDS (NAPWA) noted that AIDS service organizations were making "valiant efforts" to serve people from hotel rooms and makeshift offices. But despite the strong local response, NAPWA said the federal Department of Health and Human Services had yet to announce a plan to guarantee HIV-positive evacuees access to antiretroviral medication and medical care. This, even after NAPWA sent a September 2, 2005, letter to Secretary Leavitt of the Department of Health and Human Services, offering help in light of the vulnerable position of tens of thousands of HIV positive men and women in the impacted area.

The Lambda Legal Defense and Education Fund (LLDEF) created the "Survivor Rights after Hurricane Katrina Fact Sheet," to help those affected by the storm who experienced discrimination based on their sexual orientation, gender identity, or HIV status—including disrespect for their family members. People seeking help were directed to contact the group's toll-free national hotline or to visit its regional office in Atlanta.

Based on lessons learned after the September 11 attacks, LLDEF pressed both public and private agencies to accord lesbian and gay survivors who had lost a partner the same rights they would to those who had lost a husband or wife. The group learned how important it is to insist that relief agencies treat all people in need with compassion and to ensure that those agencies do not discriminate on the basis of sexual orientation, marital status, gender identity, or HIV status, since tragedy does not. The fact sheet listed examples of such discrimination, including the following:

> Being kept out of or being mistreated by a shelter or other facility because of your sexual orientation, gender identity or HIV status.
>
> Denied access to needed HIV medications or care.
>
> Denied help, services or the ability to assert legal rights because you are (or were) in a same-sex relationship and not married.
>
> Kept from your children or other family members, or denied the ability to take action on their behalf because you don't have a formal legal relationship.
>
> Asked to provide documents to prove your relationship or ownership of property when married people are not.
>
> Turned away or mistreated by a private or public relief agency based on religious views about LGBT or HIV-affected people.
>
> Mistreated in temporary or permanent foster care.
>
> Denied the right to handle the affairs of a deceased loved one.

LLDEF demanded that everyone affected by Hurricane Katrina living in a shelter or other temporary housing must be safe and treated with equal respect, and no one should be subjected to discriminatory exclusion, intimidation, or violence. "Tragedy does not discriminate, and neither should relief agencies," said Kevin Cathcart, executive director of LLDEF in a September 12, 2005 press release.

The National Youth Advocacy Coalition, a LGBT youth group based in Washington, DC, created the Hurricane Katrina LGBT Relief Fund in partnership with other organizations around the country. The fund mobilized to raise money for Gulf

Coast LGBT groups to ensure that LGBT youth and families, facing unique vulnerabilities, received the critical support they needed to regain stability in their lives.[4]

The Center for Artistic Revolution (CAR) in Little Rock, Arkansas, helped LGBT Katrina evacuees in the state.[5] Arkansas had the second-largest number of relocated hurricane evacuees, and CAR had the wisdom to recognize that a number of them would be LGBT people. The group created a resource base of LGBT Arkansans and allies who offered housing and other help. It located LGBT evacuees and helped them obtain the resources they needed, and also helped them with any feelings of isolation they might have been experiencing.

CAR's response was a snapshot of just how much national, regional, state, and local LGBT groups were carefully monitoring the situation of LGBT people affected by Katrina. Important coverage was provided by local, southern, regional, and national LGBT papers such as the *Houston Voice*, the Atlanta-based *Southern Voice*, and the DC-based *Washington Blade*. They were joined by the LGBT community Web site PlanetOut.

It didn't take long for stories to circulate about how gays, lesbians, and transgender people were being mistreated at locations that opened their doors to Hurricane Katrina evacuees. The story of Arpollo Vicks made national news. Vicks, a transgender woman, barely escaped with her life by swimming to safety when Hurricane Katrina floodwaters engulfed her New Orleans home. She slept on a highway for two days before she and her two teenage nieces were bused to a shelter in Bryan, Texas, about 100 miles north of Houston. Once reaching Houston, Vicks endured yet another ordeal. She was tossed in jail for six days and separated from her family for taking a shower. Her treatment prompted advocacy groups to mobilize around the legal needs—in addition to humanitarian needs—of LGBT citizens who were suffering in the aftermath of Katrina.

Vicks, who goes by the name Sharlie, had used the women's shower at the Texas A&M University-run evacuee shelter. When another woman complained to authorities that it made her "uncomfortable," university police arrested Vicks for trespassing, according to Mara Keisling, executive director of the National Center for Transgender Equality (NCTE). "They took a person and put her into basically solitary confinement for a week after she had just lost everything," Keisling told PlanetOut. "And I am just aghast that that kind of thing happens in America."

Under pressure from individuals and organizations around the country, the authorities eventually released Vicks from jail and dropped the charges.[6] The Red Cross moved her to a hotel in Houston, where she was reunited with her nieces and her mother. But Keisling said she still worried about others whose rights may have been trampled during the crisis.

What happed to Vicks underscored the urgent need to make all shelters safe for transgender people and led the NCTE to create the fact sheet "Making Shelters Safe for Transgender Evacuee."[7] It also published *Transitioning Our Shelters: A Guide to Making Homeless Shelters Safe for Transgender People.* This important document has been distributed post-Katrina to major shelter managers such as the Red Cross and the Salvation Army as well as to transgender support groups and the LGBT community centers in relevant geographic areas.

A major element of these documents is public education. The storm represented an opportunity to inform people that transgender people identify as or express a gender that is different from their sex at birth. They include people who are born male but live as female, or vice versa, and also people who are androgynous. All transgender people are at significant risk of harassment and physical or sexual assault by people who do not understand, are fearful of, or do not approve of them. This work advocated for evacuation shelters that are safe for transgender people (like other evacuees, they have nowhere else to go) and that can meet the unique difficulties they face in this time of crisis. It is not difficult to ensure safe shelter for transgender people.

Here are some of the guidelines that the NCTE fact sheet offered:

*Respect a person's self-identification as male or fe-
male.* According to the National Coalition for the
Homeless, if someone identifies herself as a woman,
she should be treated as a woman in all circumstances,
regardless of whether she was born male and regardless of whether she has had sex reassignment surgery.
A person's stated identity should be recognized
and respected, and shelter staff/volunteers should
use the name and pronoun ("he" or "she") that the
person prefers. If you don't know which term to use,
ask politely.

*Understand that people may not have updated identifi-
cation.* Evacuees who fled their homes in crisis may
not have identification that correctly identifies their
gender or the name they use. The gender and name
a person provides should be respected and used,
regardless of the name and gender listed on their
documents.

*Respect a person's evaluation of what housing options
are safe or unsafe for that person.* Transgender people
should be allowed to choose the housing option
that they believe is the safest for them. Generally, if
shelters are sex-segregated, people who identify as
men should be housed with men, and people who
identify as women should be housed with women.
This is true regardless of whether people have identification showing this name/gender, regardless
of whether they look masculine or feminine, and
regardless of whether they've had sex reassignment
surgery. However, a person's own evaluation of
his or her safety should always be respected. For
example, transgender men (born female) may feel
safer housed with women. Shelters should also offer transgender residents the ability to sleep within
eyesight/earshot of the night staff to lower the risk
of assault and harassment.

*Respond to inappropriate behavior or harassment by
any person.* Harassment of any person, including a
transgender person, should not be tolerated. Don't
base policies or rules on untrue stereotypes about
transgender people. It is not fair or correct to as-

sume that just because a person is transgender or has male genitals they are a physical threat to others. Enforce/make rules based only on inappropriate behaviors.

Ensure safe bathroom and shower options. Transgender people should be welcome to use bathrooms and showers that correspond to their self-identified gender or the facilities that feel safest for them. It is rarely illegal for people to use the bathroom that corresponds to the gender they identify as. And, in many places, it may be illegal to deny them access to the bathroom that corresponds to the gender they identify as. Other people's discomfort is not a valid reason to deny a transgender person access to facilities. If possible, gender-neutral bathrooms should be made available. It may be necessary to add a stall door or shower curtain to address valid privacy and safety concerns.

Understand that transgender people may not "look like" the people they feel they are. Evacuees are generally without their personal toiletries, clothing, makeup, shaving supplies, and all of the other items they typically use to groom. For example, a transgender woman (born male) may be unable to shave facial hair without her toiletries. This does not mean she should be treated with disrespect or not seen as a woman.

Keep a person's transgender status confidential, unless he or she tells you otherwise. This minimizes the risk of discrimination and violence. Transgender status is personal health information that is nobody else's business.

finding the radical right connection

Since 1993, SONG has been monitoring radical right groups with agendas that are antigay, anti-people of color, and antiwomen.[8] As a result, we are familiar with the sharp work of People for the American Way, which also monitors and reports on the radical right through its *Right Wing Watch* reports. Following

Hurricane Katrina, we were most intrigued by its report on Operation Blessing, an organization founded by televangelist Pat Robertson.[9]

Soon after the storm, the Federal Emergency Management Agency (FEMA) faced criticism for promoting a list of charities that featured Robertson's Operation Blessing among the top three "cash-only" groups (designated for anyone looking to donate money, rather than supplies or services). In addition, National Public Radio (NPR) reported that 19 of the other 21 groups on the government's widely circulated list were religious. In a Bloomberg.com report, Richard Walden of Operation USA said that FEMA's list "not only ignores secular agencies but ignores some of the best faith-based agencies like World Vision." Featuring Operation Blessing, Walden said, "gives Pat Robertson millions of extra dollars." He describes the list as "a departure from how the administration has handled previous disasters. To my knowledge, they have never done it before with such a narrowly focused list of religious groups, some of whom are not known for being relief groups."[10] According to NPR, pledges to Operation Blessing for the Katrina relief effort at that time approached $200 million—close to the amount raised by relief organizations in the ten days following the September 11 attacks.

In the *New York Daily News*, Juan Gonzalez provided some background on Pat Robertson's Operation Blessing. In 1999, Virginia attorney general Mark Earley concluded that although Robertson had raised millions from viewers of his *700 Club* television show to aid Rwandan refugees, the Operation Blessing "humanitarian" supply planes had been used primarily to transport mining equipment to a Robertson-owned diamond mine. Last year, the largest US recipient of Operation Blessing's charitable donations was Robertson's own Christian Broadcasting Network, which produces *The 700 Club*. It was on this program, on August 22, 2005, that Robertson called for the assassination of Venezuelan president Hugo Chavez and led viewers in prayer for Supreme Court vacancies "one way or the other." On September 7, 2005, *Christian Today* reported that as part of its Katrina relief efforts, Operation Blessing, along with Campus Crusade for Christ, had placed an order for 80,000 bibles from the World Bible Translation Center.[11]

We cannot allow those opposition forces to use catastrophic events like Hurricane Katrina to continue to further their agenda.

endnotes

1   SONG is active in a region that encompasses 12 southern states: Alabama, Arkansas, Florida, Georgia, Kentucky, Louisiana, Mississippi, North Carolina, South Carolina, Tennessee, Virginia, and West Virginia.

2   Their founding statement, released on September 15, 2005, reads:

> In the wake of the worst natural disaster in the history of the United States, intensified by atrophic, criminal government neglect and racist repression, Community Labor United—a seven-year-old New Orleans-based coalition dedicated to creating spaces for grassroots organizations to engage in dialogue, strategic planning, and building collective work—has been facilitating the development of a People's Hurricane Relief Fund and Reconstruction Oversight Committee.

3   Some of the community-based groups working on the ground in the Gulf Coast states include Community Labor United, the People's Hurricane Fund, Critical Resistance Louisiana, Federation of Child Care Centers of Alabama, the Louisiana Coalition Against Domestic Violence, the Louisiana Environmental Network, the Mississippi Low-Income Child Care Initiative, and the Mississippi Workers Center for Human Rights-Southern Relief Workers Fund.

4   Signers included the National Gay and Lesbian Task Force, the Human Rights Campaign, the National Center for Lesbian Rights, the National Black Justice Coalition, the Mautner Project, the National Federation of LGBT Community Centers, the Federation of LGBT Organizations, the Metropolitan Community Church, Children of Lesbian and Gays Everywhere, the Family Pride Coalition, and the National Center for Transgender Equality.

5   CAR, a 501(c)(3) sponsored, multi-issue, grassroots, statewide organization, works to promote and achieve a just and peaceful society that respects the value of *all* people living in Arkansas.

6   Pressure was exerted by university faculty, local transgender people and allies, the Montrose Counseling Center, Phyllis Frye and her law firm, and also the Lesbian and Gay Lobby of Texas, Lambda Legal Defense and Education Fund, the Human Rights Campaign, the National Gay and Lesbian Task Force, and the Sylvia Rivera Law Center of New York.

7   The fact sheet was published by the Lambda Legal Defense and Education Fund, the National Gay and Lesbian Task Force, and the National Center for Transgender Equality.

8   These radical right groups include Christian Coalition, Focus on the Family, the Concerned Women of America, the Family Research Council, and the Traditional Values Coalition.

9   According to the Operation Blessing website, http://www.ob.org/, Operation Blessing International Relief and Development Corporation (OBI) is a nonprofit 501 (c)(3) humanitarian organization based in Virginia Beach, Virginia. Since 1978, OBI has touched the lives of more than 184 million people in 96 countries and all 50 states, providing goods and services valued at more than $1.1 billion. OBI is governed by a national board of directors that includes founder M. G. "Pat" Robertson. OBI is a member of the Association of Evangelical Relief and Development Organizations and is registered with the Federal Emergency Management Association and the United States Agency for International Development.

10   Heidi Przybyla, "Bush Administration Charity List Dominated by Religious Groups," *Bloomberg.com*, September 2, 2005, http://www.bloomberg.com/apps/news?pid=10000087&sid=a.YafP.BwkJA&refer=top_world_news.

11   Maria Mackay, "100,000 Bibles to be Sent to Survivors of Hurricane Katrina," *Christiantoday.com*, September 8, 2005, www.christiantoday.com/news/missions/100000.bibles.to.be.sent.to.survivors.of.hurricane.katrina/486.htm.

this is criminal
malik rahim

It's criminal. From what you're hearing, the people trapped in New Orleans are nothing but looters. We're told we should be more "neighborly." But nobody talked about being neighborly until after the people who could afford to leave…left.

If you ain't got no money in America, you're on your own. People were told to go to the Superdome, but they have no food, no water there. And before they could get in, people had to stand in line for 4–5 hours in the rain because everybody was being searched one by one at the entrance.

I can understand the chaos that happened after the tsunami, because they had no warning, but here there was plenty of warning. In the three days before the hurricane hit, we knew it was coming and everyone could have been evacuated.

We have Amtrak here that could have carried everybody out of town. There were enough school buses that could have evacuated 20,000 people easily, but they just let them be flooded. My son watched 40 buses go underwater—they just wouldn't move them, afraid they'd be stolen.

People who could afford to leave were so afraid someone would steal what they own that they just let it all be flooded. They could have let a family without a vehicle borrow their extra car, but instead they left it behind to be destroyed.

There are gangs of white vigilantes near here riding around in pickup trucks, all of them armed, and any young black they see who they figure doesn't belong in their community, they shoot him. I tell them, "Stop! You're going to start a riot."

When you see all the poor people with no place to go, feeling alone and helpless and angry, I say this is a consequence of HOPE VI. New Orleans took all the HUD money it could get to tear down public housing, and families and neighbors who'd relied on each other for generations were uprooted and torn apart.

Most of the people who are going through this now had already lost touch with the only community they'd ever known. Their community was torn down and they were scattered. They'd already lost their real homes, the only place where they knew everybody, and now the places they've been staying are destroyed.

But nobody cares. They're just lawless looters—dangerous.

The hurricane hit at the end of the month, the time when poor people are most vulnerable. Food stamps don't buy enough but for about three weeks of the month, and by the end of the month everyone runs out. Now they have no way to get their food stamps or any money, so they just have to take what they can to survive.

Many people are getting sick and very weak. From the toxic water that people are walking through, little scratches and sores are turning into major wounds.

People whose homes and families were not destroyed went into the city right away with boats to bring the survivors out, but law enforcement told them they weren't needed. They are willing and able to rescue thousands, but they're not allowed to.

Every day countless volunteers are trying to help, but they're turned back. Almost all the rescue that's been done has been done by volunteers anyway.

My son and his family—his wife and kids, ages one, five, and eight—were flooded out of their home when the levee broke. They had to swim out until they found an abandoned building with two rooms above water level.

There were 21 people in those two rooms for a day and a half. A guy in a boat who just said "I'm going to help regardless" rescued them and took them to Highway 10 and dropped them there.

They sat on the freeway for about three hours, because someone said they'd be rescued and taken to the Superdome. Finally they just started walking, had to walk six and a half miles.

When they got to the Superdome, my son wasn't allowed in—I don't know why—so his wife and kids wouldn't go in. They kept walking, and they happened to run across a guy they knew with a tow truck, and he gave them his own personal truck.

When they got here, they had no gas, so I had to punch a hole in my gas tank to give them some gas, and now I'm trapped. I'm getting around by bicycle.

People from Plaquemines Parish were rescued on a ferry and dropped off on a dock near here. All day they were sitting on the dock in the hot sun with no food, no water. Many were in a daze; they've lost everything.

They were all sitting there surrounded by armed guards. We asked the guards could we bring them water and food. My mother and all the other church ladies were cooking for them, and we have plenty of good water.

But the guards said, "No. If you don't have enough water and food for everybody, you can't give anything." Finally the people were hauled off on school buses from other parishes.

You know Robert King Wilkerson (the only one of the "Angola 3" political prisoners who's been released). He's been back in New Orleans working hard, organizing, helping people. Now nobody knows where he is. His house was destroyed. Knowing him, I think he's out trying to save lives, but I'm worried.

The people who could help are being shipped out. People who want to stay, who have the skills to save lives and rebuild are being forced to go to Houston.

It's not like New Orleans was caught off guard. This could have been prevented.

There's military right here in New Orleans, but for three days they weren't even mobilized. You'd think this was a third world country.

I'm in the Algiers neighborhood of New Orleans, the only part that isn't flooded. The water is good. Our parks and schools could easily hold 40,000 people, and they're not using any of it.

This is criminal. These people are dying for no other reason than the lack of organization.

Everything is needed, but we're still too disorganized. I'm asking people to go ahead and gather donations and relief supplies but to hold on to them for a few days until we have a way to put them to good use.

I'm challenging my party, the Green Party, to come down here and help us just as soon as things are a little more organized. The Republicans and Democrats didn't do anything to prevent this or plan for it and don't seem to care if everyone dies.

Malik's phone is working. He welcomes calls from old friends and anyone with questions or ideas for saving lives.

the birth of the clinic:
action medics in new orleans
roger benham

Since the height of the antiglobalization movement in 2001, I've been involved with a loose affiliation of political activists with first aid training known as "action medical." Its roots go back to the civil rights movement of the early 1960s, when medical and nursing students provided emergency care to marchers attacked by police on the road to Selma. Carrying basic supplies, trained by peers, and working within well-defined skill limits, action medics have cared for activists suffering medical emergencies, injuries, and illness on city streets and in forest defense camps. Drawing heavily from the protocols of wilderness medicine, action medics work within areas that may be inaccessible to standard emergency medical services, using makeshift materials and assuring patients of their anonymity and privacy. In many places, emergency medical services have rules against entering areas that are "unsecured" by the police. When a group of people are being attacked by the police, or are holding an intersection or a blockade against the orders of the police, that area is definitely "unsecured." In such situations, action medics can work where an ambulance cannot enter.

Action medics are explicitly political and partisan. Rather than offering care unconditionally and acquiescing to police orders, we act as advocates for our patients, and, in my view, as active support networks. We treat illness and injury so that our patients can accomplish their goals; we exist to enable direct actions to succeed.

During the course of my work as an action medic, I've pursued additional training and experience, becoming certified as a wilderness emergency medical technician and a first aid instructor, and volunteering with the Union of Palestinian Medical Relief Committees, a nongovernmental organization in the West Bank. In the summer of 2005, my wife, Heather, and I took extended leaves from our jobs in New England and worked with Mountain Justice Summer, a campaign in southern Appalachia against mountaintop-removal coal mining. For two months, we lived in rural West Virginia and in East Tennessee, organizing and treating campaigners' injuries and sicknesses. At the end of August, we returned to New England, just before Hurricane Katrina swept ashore from the Gulf. As the levees crumbled and New Orleans was abandoned, as the racism of the governmental response became obvious to even the corporate media, Heather and I sat by our radio, amazed. If only we had stayed in the South, perhaps we could have been part of relief operations in some small way.

Five days after the storm, Ryan, an anarchist musician whom I'd worked with before, called me. He was organizing benefit concerts for action medics going to the Gulf Coast. Was I going to go? he asked. A Food Not Bombs (FNB) bus would be leaving from Hartford. A national network committed to feeding the homeless healthy vegetarian foods in public places, Food Not Bombs activists were experienced in making do with recycled materials and found objects. The Hartford folks had collected a ton of donated food and clothing in a few short days, from people from around the area who ached to help in some way. They carried on the bus a mobile field kitchen with the capability of cooking several hundred meals a day.

On September 6, I jumped on the FNB bus with a backpack of medical supplies and several hundred dollars that had been donated to me by friends and neighbors. On the road, I called Noah Morris and Scott Mechanic, action medics and old friends. They were driving southward with Jamie "Bork"

Laughner, an activist from Washington, DC, and had been in contact with Malik Rahim.

Malik, a New Orleans native, lives with his partner, Sharon Johnson, in the neighborhood of Algiers, and had stayed throughout Katrina. A perennial Green Party candidate for city council and former Black Panther, Malik had broadcast his phone number and a call for help over a number of progressive radio networks. Algiers was under an advisory evacuation, not the mandatory one in place in the rest of the city. Most residents had fled, but some remained, mainly elderly and poor. The National Guard had been abusive, power was out, and white vigilantes roamed the streets, hunting "looters." No medical aid had arrived.

Working their own contacts, my companions from Food Not Bombs learned that a Veterans for Peace convoy, traveling eastward at the end of August from Camp Casey, the antiwar protest outside George Bush's ranch in Texas, had been caught by Katrina in Covington, Louisiana, just across Lake Pontchartrain from New Orleans. They'd been feeding survivors all over southeast Louisiana since then, having established a relief center before the Red Cross ever deployed.

In the early morning hours of September 8, the Hartford bus rendezvoused with Noah, Scott, and Bork at a Nashville rest stop. Their van was loaded with donations from DC and medical supplies from Mountain Justice Summer they'd picked up along the way. Late that night, the bus and the van pulled into the Veterans for Peace camp in Covington. They'd driven one vanload of supplies to Malik and Sharon that day, and Noah, Bork, Scott, and I made plans to convoy in the morning. After a few hours' sleep, we got moving. We passed through a military checkpoint and crossed Lake Pontchartrain on the 22–mile-long causeway. Because the city was encouraging everyone to leave, we were very apprehensive about being able to get in. We were careful to hide any sign that we were encouraging people to stay and rebuild; our story was that we were going in to render emergency assistance to a few friends, not that we planned on staying and helping residents to also render emergency services as well. Across the waters of the lake, Chinook helicopters hauled slings of sand for patching the levees, and the skyscrapers of New Orleans' central business district stood above the water. Stretching away to the east and west were the lakeshore and miles of drowned houses.

Algiers is on the west bank of the Mississippi, directly across the river from the French Quarter and the Ninth Ward. We tried the most direct route first, which would have taken us through downtown, but we were stopped at another checkpoint on the Orleans Parish line. There was no arguing our way through here, cover story or not. The military was allowing no one into the still-flooded areas of the east bank.

Turned back, we circled around the city to the west, crossed the river, and approached Algiers along the west bank. We made it though this route's checkpoint with a minimum of trouble. Though, the day before at the same checkpoint, a convoy of black medical professionals from Georgia was turned back.

We pulled up in front of Malik and Sharon's house at noon. Malik had gotten permission to set up a clinic in Masjid Bilal, the mosque he once attended. The streets were covered with shingles, fallen trees, and downed utility lines. Abandoned dogs, many of them pit bulls, hungry and mean, foraged in piles of rubble. A decomposed human body lay in front of the neighborhood's community center. Dozens of helicopters filled the sky. The tower and flight deck of the amphibious assault ship USS *Iwo Jima* loomed above the levee, moored in the middle of the river, as if in a combat zone. Infantry squads patrolled the streets, assault rifles at the ready.

At the mosque, Malik and I laid tarps over the floor of the musalla, the sanctuary where you'd normally have to remove your shoes. Rfuah and Ilonda, two activists from the neighborhood, helped us unload and organize our meager supplies. They told us what it had been like, how their houses had sustained roof damage and all their possessions had gotten soaked by Katrina's driving rains. They and their families, who ran a community center and were longtime activists, had been managing the best they could through it all, helping their neighbors, working around the National Guard and the white vigilantes who were lording it over the remaining Algerines without any oversight or outside contact. They had been working to hold their shattered neighborhood together, without any help. And now they were exhausted.

Curfew came at 4 p.m. The streets were patrolled by infantry in trucks and Humvees. We slept on the floor of the mosque.

We opened the doors that next morning at 7 a.m. I shouldered a bag of medical supplies and walked down the street with Ilonda, looking for people whom she knew or suspected were still around, mainly elders with no means to evacuate. Many were suffering the effects of poverty and oppression. Diabetes, heart disease, high blood pressure, and other diseases related to or exacerbated by substandard health care, lack of access to healthy foods, and toxins in the environment afflicted far too many residents of Algiers. These were conditions that predated the hurricane.

Walking back to the mosque, I met a squad of soldiers talking to Noah, Scott, and Bork. The soldiers wanted to know how I was getting into people's houses. Under orders to conduct a census of survivors, they were frustrated by people's hiding from them. Well, we explained, we were invited by people from the neighborhood. We didn't carry weapons, and we weren't trying to get people to evacuate. "We're anarchists," Bork said, and the soldiers' eyebrows went up. I cringed—we hadn't agreed among ourselves about how we would present ourselves to the authorities. However, we never experienced any negative effects from making our political affiliations public. Unlike experiences we'd all had with police forces, who usually treated anarchists as terrorists, or at least terrorist suspects, most of our interactions with the uniformed military in New Orleans were remarkably cordial. There was some real anger among the regular army troops about what had happened to New

Orleans. The New Orleans Police Department (NOPD) was another story. Corrupt and brutal before the storm, when they showed up again on the streets of Algiers about September 16, they were abrupt, angry, and threatening, waving riot shotguns around and menacing people.

We didn't want uniformed men with guns—friendly or hostile—around a first aid station, so we scrawled a large sign and hung it by the door: No Weapons, Including Police and Military.

A steady stream of people had been coming into the mosque that first morning. Some needed first aid for cuts and injuries like broken toes untreated since the storm, but most needed prescription medications. Many were older men, of whom many were veterans and were suffering from high blood pressure, diabetes, and heart disease. Some had been receiving medications in the mail from the Veterans Administration (VA); others had been getting their health care at Charity Hospital in downtown New Orleans. But in the wake of Katrina, the VA and the US postal service were nonexistent, and Charity Hospital had been destroyed by the flood. Prescriptions had run out. Blood pressures had risen to levels that were, in some cases, life threatening. These patients should have been taken immediately to a pharmacy or a hospital, but there were none to be taken to. If someone were to have a stroke, diabetic emergency, or heart attack, there was no ambulance to call.

We asked soldiers what could be done to help these men, how we could fill their prescriptions. The only answer the army had was to evacuate them—to take them to the infamous Ernest N. Morial Convention Center across the river, then to the airport, and fly them out, dispersed across the country, to wherever the already discredited FEMA process happened to send them, with no idea of when or if they'd be able to return.

We needed nurses, doctors, and drugs. We needed to create a real clinic, and fast, or New Orleans would lose more people, people it could not afford to lose. We were not just providing medical relief; we were starting to provide basic health care to a community that had been historically underserved, so that people could save their homes and neighborhoods from extinction. With the East Bank of the city under mandatory evacuation, Algiers, on the West Bank, could be a progressive beachhead for reclaiming New Orleans for its people, and a point of resistance against gentrification and ethnic cleansing. Having evolved as a support network for those seeking social change, action medics had to adapt to becoming a support network for those fighting to preserve their community.

Under the state of emergency declared just before Katrina, physicians from out of state were given authorization to treat people in Louisiana. Doctors from around the country who were involved in antiwar work were pouring into the Veterans for Peace encampment in Covington. On September 10, the clinic's second day, we began to phone in pharmaceutical needs to these doctors from patients' empty bottles, and they organized a full vanload of refills. We waited, rendering first aid.

Several hours later, Homeland Security called Noah. They asked some very strange questions about our drug shipment. Had that remark about us being anarchists already been passed along the chain of command? Were we being constantly monitored, and might we be getting a visit from them soon? Since many of our anarchist comrades had had just such visits under "normal" American conditions, we had good reason to think it might happen to us.

The actual reason for the call was something different, yet equally outrageous. The driver bringing our supplies—a licensed practical nurse from Texas, who had been working with Veterans for Peace and the Red Cross for two weeks—was detained by police for 12 hours. The driver was eventually released, but the drugs disappeared. People in New Orleans would have to wait another two days to get their meds.

In emergency response trainings, I've been taught never to self-deploy (to act on one's own initiative, without orders from the established chain of command) to the site of a disaster, that self-deployed first responders endanger survivors and hinder relief. Yet time and again in Louisiana, we saw official relief efforts hinder direct, possibly lifesaving care and never witnessed the reverse.

Malik and Sharon had some bicycles neighbors had given them. We taped handmade signs with the mosque's address on the back and canvassed the neighborhood, checking in with people sitting on their front porches. Constantly, we were stopped by the military. Sometimes it was a new unit asking who we were; sometimes they would refer us to people who needed medical care. The idea of EMTs on bicycles was initially a shock to the GIs with their trucks and Humvees. I wondered what their morning briefings were like, after Bork had handed them literature about gentrification and capitalist redevelopment plans. They soon were referring to us as "the Panther clinic" or "the anarchist clinic."

Without advanced certifications or drugs, we administered herbal treatments. The use of herbs, traditional Chinese medicine, homeopathy, acupuncture, and other non-Western methods of healing has always been a basic part of action medical philosophy, alongside the best standards of what Americans now think of as "regular" health care. We also distributed large quantities of donated vitamins, personal hygiene products, and condoms. More arrived every day, driven to Algiers by progressive activists from across the country, and beyond.

On September 11, we were called by members of a French relief group, *Secours Populaire*. They had heard about us at a meeting of activists in Baton Rouge they had attended. "We're not affiliated with any government or Red Cross work," I emphasized. "We're activists."

"We know what you are, and that's why we want to come help you," they replied.

Several hours later, Anna, Pierre, and Monique, a physician from Paris, arrived in a truck full of supplies. To our surprise, they told us that no one else was doing work like ours anywhere in south Louisiana. There were many distribution centers, run by the Red Cross and various faith-based groups, the army was doing some health care out of mobile clinics, and some local residents with training had performed phenomenal work in the first weeks after the storm, but no one was staying put in one place, actively bringing other volunteers into the area to provide primary health care on an indefinite basis. As they accompanied me on house calls, they were amazed at people's poor health. Chronic illnesses, old untreated injuries, and results of neglect had only been exacerbated by Katrina, not created by it.

Soon Scott Weinstein, an action medic and nurse from Quebec who'd been working out of Baton Rouge with the government relief effort, arrived, hitching a ride on an ambulance. He told us the unarmed ambulance crew had been afraid to drive into Algiers. We were apparently working in a very dangerous combat zone. It was news to us, sitting outside between patients and exchanging jokes and sea stories with Norman, an ex-merchant seaman who lived across the street, and Yogi, the octogenarian World War II vet from around the corner.

On September 13, members of the action medical collective in the Bay Area arrived from California, including one medical doctor, Michael Kozart. Michael was a medical doctor, which enabled us to finally begin prescribing medication on-site. We began keeping patient records and storing them according to confidentiality standards and federal law.

We soon extended our house calls to the other side of the river. Food Not Bombs had established its kitchen at a local activists' home in the Bywater area of the Ninth Ward. They directed us to people they had found who still held out, in the Ninth Ward, in Central City, and in the Seventh Ward. Everywhere, people had formed small groups to get themselves and their neighbors through the storm and its aftermath. We started bringing them water and putting Malik and others in touch with them. We began receiving shipments of vital vaccinations against waterborne and contagious diseases like hepatitis and tetanus. Soon even the New Orleans Fire Department and the Sewage and Levee Board were sending their workers to us. Medical volunteers who had been sitting in Baton Rouge, awaiting official instructions, began showing up to work. Returning New Orleanians became involved, alongside health care volunteers from elsewhere.

As I write this a year later, in August 2006, the first aid station has become the Common Ground Health Clinic, a permanent presence in the Orleans Parish health care system, a system still severely damaged.

Mobile clinics have been set up at relief centers throughout southeast Louisiana. The Latino Health Outreach Project, a locally initiated spinoff of the Common Ground Health Clinic, services the undocumented workers who began arriving in October in search of work on the reconstruction effort. It offers vaccinations and primary health care and serves as a health and social services advocate. Hundreds of doctors, medical students, nurses, herbalists, acupuncturists, EMTs, and first-aiders from around the world have volunteered. More than 60,000 people have been treated.

The networks, planning, and contacts established through years of hard work in many places enabled us to answer needs neglected by the government. From Mountain Justice Summer and other environmental campaigns, we had contacts throughout the South, a ready source of medical supplies, and an ability to work far from modern infrastructure. From our activist work over the years, we had built a rolodex of progressive media contacts. From longtime community activists, we had local contacts and access to neighborhood resources, like the Masjid Bilal mosque. From Food Not Bombs, we had transportation, supplies, and a resourceful willingness to make do with found materials. From solidarity work in places like Palestine, we had experience interacting with soldiers in war zones. From Veterans for Peace, we had dedicated activists and infrastructure. From action medical, we had the skills, certifications, and experience that made it possible to practice medicine in unsecured areas without guns.

Most of all, from our politics we had the ability to treat the courageous, resourceful survivors of Hurricane Katrina as friends, comrades, and equals.

There have been problems and limitations. No matter how hard we worked or how many donations we received, our efforts could never match the lack of effort on the part of the government. It was sometimes easy to become intoxicated with how much was accomplished with so little, but we should be realistic. We cannot perform helicopter rescues, evacuate large numbers of people, or deal with thousands of hospital patients and nursing home residents, as the official response did in the first days of September, however belatedly or badly. We cannot build levees that can withstand storm surges, or restore wetlands that have been lost, and which would have provided additional protection. These are all larger social functions that require the mobilization of large-scale resources. We cannot, in some separate activist milieu, deal with the national problem of racism that Katrina showed to all of us. Racism is something we are constantly called upon to deal with in our smaller community as well. In the months after the storm, it became a problem that so many predominantly white activists were able to flock to New Orleans to work, while so many black New Orleanians did not have the means to do so and remained stranded in their diaspora. Many community activists from Louisiana became frustrated with the privilege and ignorance exhibited by volunteers who came from outside the state. Some might view our initial response in September as the beginning of this dynamic.

In an age of global climate chaos, imperialist war, and corporate supremacy, New Orleans is only the beginning. Those who value justice, equality, and our planet's future must not only work to change policy at governmental and institutional levels but also prepare to respond to crises where coercive institutions can't or won't. The best preparation is sustained radical activism, before, during, and after catastrophic storms, whether they be named Katrina, racism, capitalism, or fear.

common ground relief
sue hilderbrand, scott crow, and lisa fithian

The Common Ground Collective emerged from the destruction left by Hurricane Katrina. The collective, also known as Common Ground Relief, is the result of many ingredients converging at the same moment in time and space. Hurricane Katrina and the levee failure dictated where and when these forces would come together, and the shape they would take. While working under a twofold strategy of providing short-term relief for victims of hurricane disasters in the Gulf Coast region and long-term support for rebuilding these communities in more just and sustainable ways, Common Ground Relief has found itself as part of a new movement, creating a parallel social infrastructure to replace the one responsible for the conditions causing this disaster.

The social crisis immediately after the storm and the absence of an effective emergency response strategy galvanized members of various social justice movements and individuals of conscience. A national call to action by a resident activist brought do-it-yourself (DIY) medics, relief workers, community organizers, computer techies, gardeners, lawyers, carpenters, musicians, journalists, and so many others to the New Orleans area. They filled the void created by federal, state, and city governments' unprecedented and catastrophic failure. Although this influx of support was a reaction to the disaster, the work itself has often been a matter of filling the shoes of a government that's gone AWOL—providing such basic public services as potable water, medical services, and garbage pickup—proactively addressing needs normally assigned to our government by way of the social contract.

Common Ground Relief's founders originally assumed that the presence of outside relief volunteers, predominantly young, white, and middle-class, would be short-term. Assistance from outsiders would be needed only until a critical mass of predominantly black and low-income residents could return to the city. However, even a year after the disaster, historically neglected neighborhoods, such as the Lower Ninth Ward, remain without electricity, water, and basic city services, leaving local people with little to return to. As a result, what started as a disaster relief effort by a small group has evolved into a sustained effort of outsider volunteers and a few residents working to rebuild the city of New Orleans with the unanswered question of "When is it time to leave?"

In its one year of existence, Common Ground Relief has grown faster than anyone could have imagined. Our growing pains have often been overwhelming and our organizational structures have suffered from our serendipitous inception. Although no one can predict what form the work will take in the coming months and years, it is valuable to pause and reflect on where we've come from, the road we've traveled, and the lessons we've learned from the journey. The example of Common Ground Relief, both in terms of what we continue to do well and what we need to improve on, can serve as a model for future organizing work.

disclaimer

The following pages do not pretend to speak for everyone who has worked with, supported, or been affected by Common Ground Relief, nor does it capture the entire story. Each person who has worked with the organization has had a unique experience and interpretation, and this analysis is only a limited perspective. Just like the organization itself, this chapter came about through fits and starts, with many hands in the mix. However, the authors take responsibility for the ideas and analysis. People who directly contributed to this chapter include Kerul Dyer, Sakura Koné, Malik Rahim, Jackie Sumell, and Scott Weinstein.

the early days

Common Ground Relief began immediately after Hurricane Katrina hit New Orleans, at one time the Confederacy's largest slave port. Once the levees failed, on August 29, the complete breakdown of government protection and assistance left residents to fend for themselves. White militias formed, terrorizing black communities. Malik Rahim, a native New Orleanian and a longtime activist and former member of the Black Panther Party, watched as armed white racists patrolled the streets in his neighborhood of Algiers. Concerned for the safety of his family and neighbors, on September 3, Malik put out calls for support by phone and through the black newspaper *San Francisco Bay View*. The calls were quickly picked up by other news sources. Answering the call were two white activists and friends from Austin, Texas, scott crow and Brandon Darby. While driving into New Orleans, scott noticed that only white-skinned folks were being allowed through military checkpoints. He realized that the privileges afforded them by the color of their skin would become a valuable tool in the effort to funnel resources into the devastated communities.

On the night of September 6, while sitting around the kitchen table, Malik, New Orleans resident Sharon Johnson, and scott discussed what to do next. Malik and scott had been working together for about five years on prison solidarity work. They spoke of the immediate work necessary for survival—securing and delivering food, water, and medicine—but they also saw an opportunity to build a social infrastructure that had been missing even before the storm. They discussed building an organization that would be taken over by residents. The idea of community empowerment, as opposed to the large-scale relief efforts by FEMA and the Red Cross, was an exciting one. They imagined an organization to overcome race, class, and religion, to aid and rebuild. Both had varied networks from around the country and years of organizing experience to call upon, so on September 8, Malik and scott put out another national call, one that included specific needs, such as people, medical supplies, and money, that would help realize their vision. From that point, they began the rudimentary programs that would grow into a system of support including medical clinics, distribution centers, house-gutting services, and other ad hoc tasks related to recovery.

Among the first to answer the calls for support were three first-responder street medics (known for their presence at political mobilizations) and a homeless advocate. They opened an emergency clinic on September 9, eleven days after the storm. It was the first nonmilitary-run clinic to open after the hurricane. Working out of Masjid Bilal, a local mosque in Algiers, volunteers provided medical services to more than 100 people a day. Even Red Cross, FEMA, and the military sent patients to the free clinic. Additionally, one of countless unexpected heroes that deserves mention is Sharon Johnson. Prior to the storm, Sharon had no community organizing experience. She had known Malik only a short time but waited out the storm with him. Given the opportunity to leave New Orleans, she chose to stay and took on many critical organizing roles, including overseeing the Common Ground distribution center and keeping the organization's financial records.

Within weeks, the organization grew from three people to twenty, from twenty to sixty. By early October, money and supplies were pouring in from individuals around the world and social justice organizations such as Veterans for Peace. Because Algiers had not flooded, Malik's yard became the hub of Common Ground Relief's operations, which included a distribution center and volunteer housing. In those early days, volunteers asked residents what was needed. The first priority, residents told them, was to clean up the rotting food and trash. The whole block was cleaned. The next priorities, residents said, were food, water, and medicine. Volunteers were able to obtain food and water from the military and from groups such as Veterans for Peace, but not the medicine. In response, volunteers were able to secure all but the medicine. "Solidarity, not charity" became our modus operandi for the work; we tried not to assume that we know what is best for a particular community. Weeks and months later, residents still directed the work by determining what was needed and by getting involved in the efforts, as opposed to outsiders setting the agenda.

According to Malik, the presence of white volunteers alleviated racial tensions and prevented a race war from breaking out in Algiers. In contrast to the racist militias who forced black residents to stay in their homes, the white volunteers of Common Ground Relief knocked on doors to offer food and medical assistance, and to listen to the stories of those who remained in the city. Initially, Malik was concerned for the safety of these volunteers because of the longstanding racial tensions in the area. However, in the end, the only danger these white outsiders faced was from the military and the New Orleans police, with its notorious history of corruption and harassment in the city. Common police practices in the wake of the storm included constant verbal and physical harassment, unjust arrests, and waving guns at residents and volunteers alike. Examples from the early days include that of a relief worker who was arrested for documenting police harassment and was threatened with having his body dumped in the Mississippi River. Another volunteer was jailed for double-parking a truck in front of the distribution center.

Although white volunteers were certainly abused by the police, their treatment does not compare to physical and psychological abuse black citizens experience at the hands of the police and white militias. For example, although members of the white militias were heard bragging about the killing of black men in Algiers, the question about why these bodies were left rotting in the streets for weeks remains unanswered. Many residents believe the reason the bodies of at least 17 black men, all of whom died of gunshot wounds after the storm, were not quickly collected was to send a message to local blacks that deadly force would be used to keep control of the situation.

After Hurricane Rita made landfall on September 24, Common Ground Relief was able to send 25 trucks with more than 30 tons of supplies to the First Nation tribes residing in the hard-hit bayou coastal areas near Houma, two trucks to the Lao temple in New Iberia, and a truck to Lake Charles. These supplies often arrived before those provided by the Red Cross and other "official" organizations. The organization sent mobile medical clinics to these and other areas for people unable to reach Red Cross shelters and other relief services. And it provided medical and food relief to more than 100 homebound individuals with chronic illnesses.

Since those early days in the trenches, Common Ground Relief has continued to evolve. Our focus has been to tactically use race and class privileges to bring resources into the city and redistribute them to the communities most in need. Our programs continue to grow and change in response to the changing needs of the community, as expressed by the members of the community.

Common Ground Relief has attracted more than 10,000 volunteers from all 50 states, the District of Columbia, and abroad. Its work has supported more than half a million people in the New Orleans area. This effort has flowed from across the globe in the form of volunteers, supplies, and camaraderie. This powerful network has the potential to become the foundation for an effective rapid support system across borders for future disasters.

Our health care services have treated more than 15,000 people through our Algiers clinic, mobile clinics, the Latino Health Outreach Project, and a health center in the Upper Ninth Ward. In addition to traditional care, our clinics offer massage, acupuncture, herbal remedies, and counseling. Work on a new clinic is underway in the Lower Ninth Ward, a project initiated and led by local residents.

Common Ground Relief has started and supported the operation of seven distribution centers in four different parishes. These centers have provided more than 120 tons of food and 100,000 gallons of water. Several of these centers are now community-run. We have tarped hundreds of roofs, cleaned and gutted more than 800 homes, 15 schools, 10 churches, and 5 day care centers, and provided some mold abatement, both through traditional methods and alternative techniques using Efficient Microbes (EM). We have cleaned dozens of streets, if not whole neighborhoods, and fixed up several community gardens to provide healthy food. We have treated more than a dozen sites through our bioremediation program to remove toxins in the soil from before and after Hurricane Katrina. Common Ground Relief has hosted several media centers, offering free phone and Internet access, computer training, a Web stream, and a radio station. It has opened several women's centers and provided temporary housing for residents. It has provided legal advocacy, including a legal clinic every Saturday since fall 2005. Other initiatives include after-school programs and tutoring, wetlands protection, replanting efforts, and workers' cooperatives.

Common Ground Relief has taken direct action in all of its work—that means taking matters into our own hands and building the structures needed for the society we believe in— without expecting the permission of the government, and often in defiance of it. We have responded to community requests for support, even if it meant a possible confrontation with police. Examples include entering and cleaning up the Martin Luther King, Jr. elementary school, blocking the demolition of hundreds of homes, supporting community-led efforts to reclaim public housing, including Survivors Village at the St. Bernard Projects. In the case of St. Augustine Church, we support the fight to keep a historically black Catholic church open.

Our resolve to take direction from the local community has generated a multitude of relationships that continue to grow.

the formation of common ground relief

Common Ground Relief formed in response to the enormity of the disaster left by Hurricane Katrina and the levee failures in New Orleans, and the inadequate response of the government and official aid organizations. Three factors were essential to its formation: a political vacuum, experienced radical organizers, and regular people ready to take action. Without all of these factors, the organization could not have flourished.

a political vacuum

The collapse of government structure at all levels, save for the military, created a political vacuum. There were few plans for a catastrophe of this magnitude, even though this scenario was predicted years ago. Without an effective relief effort ready on deck, the official government search-and-rescue workers were quickly overwhelmed. Only the military remained intact and in great force as a functioning arm of the government. Essentially, all civil services were gone.

As activists working for social change, we are accustomed to fighting the structures that hold inequalities in place. We tend to be reactive and spend the bulk of our energy pushing against state power. With the collapse of almost the entire civil infrastructure, organizers were in a position to be proactive in filling the void. The question of whether those of us who are outsiders were the appropriate ones to fill that void was frequently asked, and we walked a fine line between doing too much and too little, while always taking leadership from Malik and other involved residents. As the scope of the work expanded, each step along the way built survival and strength, hope and dignity in those neighborhoods.

experienced radical organizers

Common Ground Relief could not have formed without the experience of radical organizers, both in terms of ideology and on-the-ground organizing skills. The way in which Common Ground Relief approaches its work has been influenced by the philosophies of the Black Panther Party and the Zapatistas, which have much overlap between them. On some questions, such as the one of centralized versus decentralized power structures, these influences differ, and evidence of that can also be seen in our organizational structure. Finally, the mobilization skills of anarchist and global justice activists put many of the theories into practice.

black panther party

The philosophy and grassroots organizing tradition of the Black Panther Party, specifically the survival programs, seemed well-suited to use in the political vacuum of post-Katrina New Orleans. Malik, who had worked in the Black Panther Party, and many incoming volunteers in the early days were heavily influenced by the party's theories and organizing strategies. The party's survival programs, or as Huey P. Newton often referred to them, "survival programs pending revolution," included medical clinics, free breakfast for children, food giveaways, free clothing, pest control, sickle cell anemia testing, education, and prison support. These programs offered alternatives to the substandard services often found in black communities, and they gave people an opportunity to take control of their own lives.

The key philosophical pillars of these programs are self-determination and political activism. The idea is that if you don't have your basic needs satisfied, you can't organize and fight for your future. Or, more simply, it is hard to demand justice if you don't have enough to eat. So fulfilling those needs is a first, necessary step. From the very beginning, the intention of Common Ground Relief programs has been to offer basic services (food, shelter) that can support people's efforts to organize and reclaim their neighborhoods and lives.

zapatista influence

The influence of Zapatismo, or the philosophy of the Zapatistas, can also be seen in the way Common Ground Relief approaches its work, in particular in the language we use and in the idea of "leading by obeying."

In our work, the use of language was critical to restore hope and maintain dignity. We redefined many aspects of political language, including the traditional characterizations of oppressed peoples. Instead of making people or communities sound like statistics or one-dimensional figures that can be written off, we sought to use language and descriptions that maintained their dignity, both in our internal communications and in the media. We use language such as "historically neglected communities," "traditionally marginalized," and "impoverished communities" instead of typical language such as "poor," "black," and other variations. Our intent was to give people outside the region a picture of people who didn't need pity and paternalism, but who would get back on their feet with meaningful support.

Zapatismo taught us to ask questions rather than provide answers; it suggested that we "lead by obeying." We asked residents and local leadership what was needed or wanted instead of relying on our own preconceived ideas. Local people can best assess their own situation. And once the questions were answered, the programs or aid would be appropriate, unlike, for example, the Red Cross's 'one size fits all' approach that lacks the subtleties that individual neighborhoods need. For example, the Algiers neighborhood needed medical services because of the large remaining elderly population, so a free clinic was opened. In the Lower Ninth Ward, on the other hand, immediate house-gutting services were needed due to the lack of alternative housing in the area and the threat of demolition by the city, so the free house-gutting services were organized. Many other aspects of Zapatismo have been critical influences to our strategies and tactics, such as working with and expanding local support networks.

global justice activists

Since the mobilization against the World Trade Organization in Seattle in 1999, aka the Battle of Seattle, the most visible manifestation of resistance in the US has been mass protest, focusing mostly on the mechanisms of corporate globalization and war. At mobilizations around the world, a highly developed, decentralized organizational model has emerged—a model of how to feed and house activists coming to a city, provide legal support and medical attention, use media skills and independent media outlets to get the message out, and coordinate public opposition to government and corporate actions. This particular movement for social change has evolved in a way that is self-sufficient and transferable. Activists' experience with this anarchist/nonhierarchical organizational model was critical to filling the political vacuum left by Hurricane Katrina. These components can be seen in our work.

If we define anarchy as "an anti-authoritarian society that is based on voluntary association of free individuals in autonomous communities operating on principles of mutual aid and self-governance" (from Wikipedia), Common Ground Relief may be the largest anarchist-influenced organization in the US since the Industrial Workers of the World of the 1920s and 1930s. This does not suggest that the organization is or was *only* an anarchist-inspired effort, but that many of anarchism's principles have been woven into the fabric of our work, including mutual aid, direct action, solidarity, dual power, self-determination, autonomy, and self-defense. These principles are certainly not unique to anarchists and can be found in many other political movements and cultures, but anarchy is the reference point of many white organizers in the social justice movement.

Common Ground Relief volunteers have included activists from Food Not Bombs and Seeds for Peace, who worked to supply residents and volunteers with healthy meals. Anarchist street medics started the Common Ground Health Clinic and continue to provide medical services to volunteers. Free legal assistance is offered to residents and volunteers, and Indymedia folks help keep this story alive. A myriad of other organizations, groups, and collectives have contributed to the Common Ground effort, such as the Pagan Cluster, with their skills in meeting and decision-making facilitation, bioremediation (using biological organisms and processes to clean water and soil), permaculture (creating sustainable habitats by following nature's patterns), and forest defense activists, with their organizing and direct-actions skills.

ordinary people

Fortunately for New Orleans residents, thousands of concerned people ignored the words of Federal Emergency Management Agency (FEMA) director Michael Brown, issued the day Katrina hit the Gulf Coast: "We're grateful for the outpouring of support already, but it's important that volunteer response is coordinated by the professionals who can direct volunteers with the appropriate skills to the hardest-hit areas where they are needed most." Instead, people with valuable skills came to the Gulf Coast to assist, and Malik credits the diversity of those people for our success.

People from all walks of life and socioeconomic backgrounds responded, motivated by a common cause. At any given moment you might find yourself in a room with an environmental engineer from Austin, Texas, a street medic from Rhode Island, a transgender electrician from Philly, a teacher from San Francisco, a punk rock musician from New York, an independent reporter from Santa Cruz, a massage therapist from Arizona, an artist from Long Island, a nurse from Montana, a filmmaker from Denmark.

And one constant in the history of Common Ground Relief is the participation of community members working in partnership with outsider volunteers. Community partners included local church and mosque leaders, auto mechanics, day-care owners, teachers and others from the local neighborhoods. Other "ordinary people" working in solidarity included people that our society typically ignores, i.e. the traditionally marginalized people such as a welfare mother and her children, the so called 'gangsters', ex-prisoners, the homeless people who couldn't leave before or after the storm because they lacked resources or places to go. Common Ground Relief was created by ordinary people, both from the community and from around the country, doing ordinary work under extraordinary circumstances. And it's those people who continue the work.

contributions to the movement

Along with the on-the-ground work of its volunteers, Common Ground Relief's contributions to the broader movement for social change must also be considered part of our story. Common Ground Relief continues to radicalize volunteers, and it's creating support networks around the country. The group provides a powerful paradigm for proactive organizing.

proactive organizing

Radical movements in the US generally have little experience in building alternatives to the status quo, and are, instead stuck in a cycle of resisting the current institutions of power. Common Ground Relief's approach is proactive. It now offers evolving models influenced by various radical traditions.

The concept of building "dual power" recognizes that we must continue to resist oppressive structures but we must also create alternative institutions, to use the modern anarchist definition of an old communist term. The alternative institutions embody a greater vision and, it is hoped, will lead to a revolutionary transformation of society. Some of the projects started by Common Ground Relief volunteers, such as the workers' cooperative that trains low and unskilled workers while paying a living wage and the children's free breakfast programs, exemplify this strategy. The Common Ground Health Clinic continues to provide free health care in a community that lacked services before the storm, with three of the four paid staff coming from the community.

Common Ground Relief does not offer charity. Charity is offered by the government, through its various relief arms, and by private organizations for short-term solutions to deep-seated problems. Instead, we offer solidarity with the goal of creating permanent and sustainable solutions. As outsiders, our role is to work with residents to determine needs and use privilege to acquire resources.

radicalizing volunteers

The first wave of volunteers that arrived in New Orleans tended to be radical activists and organizers. However, over time this changed—the change was especially evident during college breaks. Volunteers working with Common Ground Relief have been predominantly young, white, and middle class. Many of these people have never been exposed to radical philosophies, nor have they taken action to directly address social ills. Common Ground Relief has consciously introduced a racial analysis of New Orleans during volunteer orientations and highlights the effects of racism during the disaster and its effects on the recovery. In their work with the organization, volunteers participate in direct action, often for the first time. When these volunteers return to their home communities, they continue the work as antiracist allies. Former volunteers have sent us articles they've written for local and school newspapers, organized fundraisers, and created Common Ground Relief chapters on their campuses. Common Ground Relief is both educating and empowering future activists and community organizers.

Common Ground's race analysis is informed by its work with the People's Institute for Survival and Beyond, a 25–year-old New Orleans-based antiracist training organization whose Undoing Racism workshop focuses on the ways race and racism function as barriers to community self-determination and self-sufficiency. The institute has partnered with Common Ground Relief to help both long- and short-term volunteers understand the racial landscape. More than 1,000 volunteers— both white and people of color—have participated in these trainings and explored issues ranging from media coverage of black people to individual internalized attitudes of inferiority and superiority. For example, why and in what contexts do white men talk louder and more often than men and women of color? The People's Institute helps us identify and begin to break our own patterns of racism. In addition, Common Ground's antiracism working group has organized weekly race-based caucuses, as well as a Community Voices program, in which residents are invited to come and speak to volunteers. Although it may be argued that indulging outsiders in personal-growth training does not serve the local community, we believe that the long-term results of this work will help overturn the societal racism that caused the disaster.

creating support networks

Networks for support on the ground in New Orleans and in communities around the country have been created both from existing grassroots networks and where none previously existed. From the beginning of our work, these informal networks have provided material aid, money, and people power. During our Thanksgiving Road Trip for Relief, Holiday Drive, and Alternative Spring Break events, people from around the country collected thousands of dollars' worth of tools and delivered it to us. Many of these people went back home and organized to send more shipments. The Student Solidarity Network, for example, was established as a vehicle for the 3,000 students who worked with Common Ground Relief during spring break of 2006 to continue to help out on their school campuses. Chapters formed around the country to raise money for the organization. Our networks include, among others, religious and social justice organizations, musicians and artists, and foreign supporters. These informal networks can be used to keep supporters current on what's happening in New Orleans, and also to mobilize people around other issues.

On the ground, we have forged alliances with many different residents and community and religious groups. Much of our work is directly supporting those trying to come home. As local groups are returning and getting reorganized, we are shifting more support to them. For example, the Mt. Carmel Baptist Church building, which was gutted, cleaned, and used for volunteer housing, has now been restored as a church. It continues to host a child care program supported by the Common Ground Kids and Community Project. In almost every area of our work, we have had the opportunity to collaborate with other groups. Together with the Safe Streets/Strong Communities coalition and Critical Resistance, we helped form the New Orleans Housing Eviction Action Team (NO HEAT) to support public housing residents. We have supported the Deep South Center for Environmental Justice on a project in New Orleans East and have tapped into a vast network of environmentally minded organizations. We have had numerous collaborations with local college students at Xavier, Loyola, and Tulane.

challenges, mistakes, and some lessons learned

Organizing Common Ground Relief has been far from easy. Through the process we have learned many lessons that can be used to further the larger movement for social change. We are a young organization, however, and some lessons will no doubt become more obvious with the passage of time. Besides a myriad of logistical problems—such as donated cars breaking down in a town with few mechanics, power outages, water shortages—the most obvious challenges to the work and the organization have been too little time for organizational development, the slow return of residents, and our own baggage of oppressive behaviors. We've met these challenges with varying degrees of success, but our experience with all of them can be used as lessons for future work.

no time for organizational development

Little time was spent in meetings to decide on organizational processes once the general philosophical framework had been established. As a result, although this was perhaps inevitable, given the magnitude of the disaster, structure and decision-making processes were unclear, and volunteers resorted to their own assumptions of how the process *should* work. The challenge was that the diversity of volunteers produced a diversity of assumptions.

With conflicting assumptions come negative repercussions. For example, we all used the word "collective" to describe the organization, but the first wave of volunteers and members of the organization had different ideas of what a collective is and how it operates. Many white anarchists came to New Orleans with a preconceived notion that collectives use consensus as the decision-making process. However, in black radical communities, the group defines itself and establishes the decision-making process collectively. This lack of clarity caused white activists to question the integrity of the decision-making process—when no process had actually been established. Meanwhile, the consensus processes brought in by white activists confused many community members, who were often unfamiliar with the 'rules' of participation.

These issues are still being sorted out. Currently, the decision-making process is a mixture of centralized and decentralized models. The big-picture decisions are made by a small group of long-term committed volunteers and the project-specific decisions are made by the people doing the work.

slow return of residents

A year after the storm, one of our greatest challenges is that residents are returning at a much slower pace than expected. As part of our vision for building alternative institutions and local power, we originally assumed that residents would replace outside volunteers. The organization would grow, and residents would guide that growth and directly make decisions on the various projects in order to fit the local community. Residents have replaced volunteers at the women's center and the health clinic, and organizers do work closely with residents who have returned, but the organization has continued to grow with the benefit of guidance from only a small core of the local community. As time goes on, we are seeing more integrated work, but the slow return of residents makes it difficult, and with so much of the community still displaced, it's hard to gauge the success of the effort to build community-run alternative institutions.

At the same time, the thousands of volunteers coming through require an enormous amount of organizing support, as well as constant orientation and training. Furthermore, the constant turnover has made building strong and consistent relationships over time more difficult.

products of society

One challenge to our work has been ourselves. The vast majority of volunteers, however social-justice oriented, are products of American society, complete with the insidious baggage of oppressive behaviors. The large number of white volunteers inevitably brings the issue of white superiority to the table—varying degrees of active and unexamined racism, directly affecting the ability to work in solidarity with a traditionally marginalized community. Those of us who are white out-of-towners constantly struggle with our role in the rebuilding process: Have we overstepped our boundaries? Are we honoring the local wisdom or assuming we know what is best? Will we know when it is time to leave?

Race is just one dimension of the interlocking forms of oppression in the United States today. We act out and grapple with—at times consciously and at other times unwittingly—other oppressive behaviors, manifestations of our relative place within the matrix of domination. We are working to educate ourselves and institute procedures for dealing with these issues within our volunteer community and with residents. Working agreements have been established to create an environment free of oppressive behavior—for example, racist, sexist, and homophobic behavior is prohibited while working with Common Ground Relief. Other tactics include conducting community forums and trainings, establishing mediation teams, separating at-risk people, and even physically removing people from the volunteer housing site who cannot abide by the agreements.

The realization that we often perpetuate oppressive behaviors serves as a reminder that anti-oppression work is lifework for the privileged few in our society. Our tendency to relax into old patterns is yet another argument for quickly establishing general procedures. If we lack models and revert back to old habits, those habits become the norm.

final thoughts

We've tried to capture the history of our organization in the year since Hurricane Katrina and point out our successes and what we've learned from our mistakes. This is only a limited accounting. There can and should be entire books written about the various aspects of this phenomenon called Common Ground Relief. Our experience here recalls the Spanish Civil War, a brief shining moment in history (also with anarchists playing a predominant role) from which many lessons have been gleaned. It is our hope that the same will be true of the successes and failures of "one organization of many" that has strived to create just and democratic societies.

This unprecedented effort is calling on all of us to learn new ways of building relationships and working with people from different cultures. We have made mistakes, but they are part of the process of creation. Putting theory into practice often produces unexpected results, but those results can lead to new insights—if we are paying attention.

We've included only a limited analysis of Common Ground Relief's impact on the community. A few key questions that we have struggled with (but didn't have the space to address here) include: Will we know when it is time to stop the flow of outside volunteers? What are the costs of having white volunteers in historically black neighborhoods versus the costs of not having them? What is the feminist analysis of the organization, specifically regarding its leadership? Does the tactic of using white privilege to funnel resources into the community serve to reinforce white privilege?

Regardless of any analysis, Common Ground Relief volunteers have contributed countless hours and in numerous ways to the rebuilding of the city of New Orleans and the surrounding areas. The fate of the region post-Katrina is still unknown. But we at Common Ground Relief know, in both our hearts and our minds, that history is in the making here and that we are making a difference.

corporate reconstruction and grassroots resistance
jordan flaherty

New Orleans was not devastated by a hurricane. The damage came from decades of brutal negligence, deficient planning, and from a stunningly slow response on the part of a local, state, and federal government that didn't care about the people of New Orleans, and still doesn't.

The government neglect and its abdication of responsibility, the images broadcast around the world of a people abandoned, and the mounting devastation all served as an opening act in a long struggle over the framework of relief and reconstruction. One side represents the corporatization, criminalization, militarization, and privatization of relief. On the other side are the people of New Orleans, historically overexploited and underserved by local and national government and politicians, fighting for community control of both the decisions and the finances behind the reconstruction of their city.

The "disaster before the disaster" that devastated this amazing city was man-made. It was birthed in institutional structures of racism, and it manifested in the crumbling infrastructure of schools and education and health care, and, later, in a hopelessly mismanaged relief and reconstruction, overseen by a confluence of forces ranging from multinational corporations to corporate relief agencies and military contractors—what some local organizers have referred to as "the disaster industrial complex."

In addition to the profiteers, and sometimes in counterbalance, there are other important outside players—from politicians, planners, think tanks, and foundations to tourists and media to the thousands of volunteers and allies from around the US who have come to the city to support the struggle. In New Orleans, these players have come together in huge numbers perhaps never seen anywhere else in the US, in a city with a unique culture and history that has captured the imagination and passions of millions.

privilege and profit

As a white male organizer who moved to New Orleans several years ago, I have personally profited from the inequality that has been intrinsic to the contours of this disaster. In everything from employment opportunities to housing to the amplification my writing has received in the national media, I have benefited from intersecting forms of privilege—privilege based on race certainly, but also based on gender, class, and geography—since moving to New Orleans, and especially post-Katrina.

In writing this piece, I want to acknowledge that in important ways it is not my own. My analysis of what has happened in New Orleans, the filter through which I have interpreted what I have seen here, has been developed through education I have received from countless hours of conversation and work with people from New Orleans, especially African American grassroots community organizers from organizations such as Safe Streets/Strong Communities coalition; INCITE! Women of Color Against Violence; Critical Resistance; the People's Institute for Survival and Beyond; and Community Labor United. The grassroots resistance that these groups have led has also inspired and educated me.

The fact that my voice has been more prominent than these other much more informed voices is a part of this disaster that must be acknowledged—black people of New Orleans have not only been killed and displaced and robbed, but also silenced.

The same people of New Orleans that the national media portrayed as murderers and animals remain silenced today. Even in the progressive media, white voices like mine have been overrepresented at the expense of black voices, and black female voices are doubly missing.

Beyond race and gender, the access I've had to networks outside of New Orleans gave me an advantage in the days following the evacuation in everything from housing and work to media exposure. As one community organizer expressed to me in the days following the storm,

> There's a difference between New Orleans residents and New Orleans natives. The voices I've heard speaking for us have been people who moved to New Orleans. Many of them are currently staying with family or friends from somewhere else. They're in a different situation. I'm from New Orleans; my family is from New Orleans. I don't have anywhere else.

the city

For those of you who have not lived in New Orleans, you have missed an incredible, glorious, vital city. A place of art, music, and dance. A place of sexuality and liberation. A 70–percent African American city where resistance to white supremacy has supported a generous, subversive, and unique culture of vivid beauty. New Orleans was, as more than one former resident has said, North America's African city. It is a city steeped in a culture that is specifically African American—from jazz, blues, and hip-hop to second lines, Mardi Gras Indians, parades, jazz funerals, and the tradition of red beans and rice on Monday nights. It was the number one African American tourist destination in the US, home to the annual Essence Festival, the Bayou Classic, and other major African American tourism draws.

New Orleans is a city and a people who have created a culture of community-based resistance. Perhaps more than anywhere else in the nation, in New Orleans people live in one neighborhood their whole lives and families live in the same community for generations. In the 2000 census, New Orleans ranked second among all cities in the US in the percentage of its population born in the state, at 83 percent (Santa Ana, California, was first; Las Vegas last). Fifty-four percent of the residents of the Lower Ninth Ward had been in their homes for ten years or more, far above the national average. It's a city that, as far back as the 1700s, had a large and active free African community, many of whom lived in the Treme neighborhood, which is still a center of black New Orleans culture and resistance.

New Orleans is a city and a people who have created a culture of liberation and resistance. It is where, in 1892, Homer Plessy and the Citizens Committee planned the direct action that brought the first (unsuccessful) legal challenge to the doctrine of "separate but equal." In 1970, when the city's police force tried to evict the New Orleans Black Panthers from the Desire housing projects, the entire community stood between the police and the Panthers, until the police were forced to back down.

Cornel West wrote the following shortly after the city was flooded:

> New Orleans has always been a city that lived on the edge...with Elysian Fields and cemeteries and the quest for paradise. When you live so close to death, behind the levees, you live more intensely, sexually, gastronomically, psychologically. Louis Armstrong came out of that unbelievable cultural breakthrough unprecedented in the history of American civilization. The rural blues, the urban jazz. It is the tragicomic lyricism that gives you the courage to get through the darkest storm. Charlie Parker would have killed somebody if he had not blown his horn. The history of black people in America is one of unbelievable resilience in the face of crushing white supremacist powers.[1]

All of this is to say that New Orleans is not just a tourist stop. New Orleans has a unique culture, one that is resilient, and with a history of community and resistance. With this current brutal dispossession, it is this culture we are in danger of losing.

the storm

On the day after Katrina's landfall, many of us still in the city felt that New Orleans had once again survived—battered and bruised, but all right. Then, over the next few days, water from broken levees rushed into the city. Relief, rescue, and repair efforts were far too little, far too late. I watched in horror from an apartment in the Mid-City neighborhood as flooding devastated my city. Like many of my neighbors, I evacuated days later, passing through an evacuee camp on the highway just outside of town.

In the camp I evacuated to, on Highway 10 near the Lake Pontchartrain Causeway, thousands of people—at least 90 percent of them black and poor—stood and squatted in mud and trash behind metal barricades, under an unforgiving sun, with heavily armed soldiers standing guard over them. When a bus would come through, it would stop at a seemingly random spot, state police would open a gap in one of the barricades, and people would rush on, with no information given about where the bus was going. Once inside, evacuees would be told where the bus was taking them. Baton Rouge, Houston, Arkansas, Dallas, or other locations. I was told that if you boarded a bus bound for Arkansas (for example), even people with family and a place to stay in Baton Rouge would not be allowed to get out of the bus as it passed through Baton Rouge. You had no choice but to go to the shelter in Arkansas. If you had people willing to come to New Orleans to pick you up, they were not allowed to come within 17 miles of the camp.

I traveled throughout the camp and spoke to Red Cross supervisors, Salvation Army workers, National Guard soldiers, and state police, and although they were friendly, no one could give me any details on when buses would arrive, how many, where they would go to, or any other information. I spoke to the several teams of journalists positioned around the camp and asked if any of them had been able to get any information from any federal or state officials on any of these questions. All of them, from German photographers to local *Fox* affiliates, complained that it was an unorganized, noncommunicative mess.

There was also no visible attempt by those running the camp to set up any sort of transparent and consistent systems, for instance, a line to get on buses, a way to register contact information or find family members, special-needs services for children and the infirm, phone services, treatment for possible disease exposure. There wasn't even a single trash can. The individual soldiers and police were friendly and polite—at least to me—but nobody seemed to know what was going on. As wave after wave of evacuees arrived, they were ushered behind the barricades onto mud and dirt and sewage, while heavily armed soldiers looked on. Because of the chaos, many people were on the side, not even trying to get on a bus. Children, people in wheelchairs, and everyone else waited in the sun by the side of the highway.

My experience in that camp left me with an indelible impression about the nature of this disaster. Everyone I spoke to had a story to tell, of a home destroyed, of swimming across town, of bodies and fights and gunshots and fear. I spoke to one young man who described escaping the Superdome in terror and swimming up to Mid-City.

While most people in the camp had no choice but to wait for whatever was given to them, my privileged status as a journalist and as a white male assisted me in escape via a ride to Baton Rouge from an Australian TV crew. From there, my privileged status as a nonnative of New Orleans and the connections I have throughout the US meant that a stay in a shelter was never a fear. Weeks later, I was back in the city. The majority of those who were in the camp with me no doubt remain exiled to this day, perhaps in a trailer camp in Baton Rouge or in Houston or somewhere even further removed.

Later, watching media coverage of the disaster, seeing how black New Orleanians were portrayed, I felt anger and dismay. The city I loved was demonized, the people criminalized, their homes stolen—a culture was in the process of being erased.

the relief

Relief organizations, while sometimes helpful, have become in many cases an integral part of the network of disaster profit. This phenomenon disaster has its roots in the structural, systematic problems of racism, corruption, deindustrialization, and neglect. Without a doubt, the Red Cross, Federal Emergency Management Agency (FEMA), religious charities, and other relief organizations are filled with well-meaning individuals and have helped many Gulf residents, but any effort at relief that does not address these structural problems actually contributes to sustaining them. In other words, they are part of the problem.

Days after my evacuation, I went to the River Road shelter in Baton Rouge as part of a project initiated by a grass-roots organization called Families and Friends of Louisiana's Incarcerated Children to help displaced New Orleans residents reconnect with loved ones who are lost in the labyrinth of the state's corrections system. Everyone I met was desperately trying to find an incarcerated sister or brother or child or other family member. Many people who were picked up for minor infractions in the days before the hurricane ended up being shipped to Angola Prison, a notorious former slave plantation in rural Louisiana. Most of the family members I spoke with just wanted to get a message to their loved ones. "Tell him that we've been looking for him, that we made it out of New Orleans, and that we love him," said an evacuated New Orleans East resident named Angela.

While Barbara Bush famously declared how fortunate the shelter residents were, in the real world, New Orleans evacuees were feeling anything but sheltered. Angela told me she'd barely slept since she arrived in the shelter system. "I sleep with one eye open," she said. "It's not safe in there." Christina Kucera, a Planned Parenthood organizer from New Orleans, described the situation further: "Issues of safety and shelter are intricately tied to gender. This has hit women particularly hard. It's the collapse of community. We've lost neighbors and systems within our communities that helped keep us safe."

For many who experienced the shelter system, abuse and revictimization were rampant. There were widespread reports of racism and discrimination in Red Cross shelters, especially in Lafayette, Lake Charles, and Baton Rouge. In September, New Orleans-based organizer Andrea Garland described to me the callous treatment she'd seen in the shelters in the Covington area. "The Red Cross has made at least $800 from fundraising, but people in this shelter can't get soap and are showering under a hose? Is that right?"

According to the online journal of Jodie Escobedo, a doctor from California who was volunteering in the Baton Rouge shelters around the same time, "Local officials, including politicians, select Red Cross personnel, and an especially well placed but small segment of the Louisiana medical community, have managed to get themselves into positions of power, where their prejudices result in the hoarding of supplies, vilification of the needy, and substandard treatment of volunteers and refugees alike."

In the year since the storm, the Red Cross has raised $1.8 billion, money we have not seen on the ground—a fact clear to even the Republican-controlled Congress. After an outcry that reached all the way to Washington, the president of the organization was forced to resign in December 2005, and months later an internal investigation led to further dismissals and potential criminal charges against some local supervisors and volunteers.

An aid worker with the relief organization Save the Children recently confessed to me that despite her organization's deep pockets, an entrenched bureaucracy meant that very little of that money was passed along to people in need. "Initiatives take forever to be approved," she said. "Sometimes so long that by the time we have the support we need, the effort has passed. There's so much money behind us we can do pretty much whatever we want and don't have to worry about funding, but instead of supporting local efforts, it feeds our own privileges."

This may go down as the most militarized "relief" effort in history. The Chicago police camped out in a bar on Bourbon

Street while an Israeli security company named Instinctive Shooting International set up on Audubon Place and the National Guard and Blackwater, a private paramilitary company, were seemingly everywhere. Meanwhile, white vigilante gangs patrolled the West Bank, with the tacit permission of local authorities. One Eighth Ward resident told me, "Why don't they send some of them with tools to rebuild instead of just weapons? I guess they don't want it rebuilt."

For months, virtually the only aid for people in the city was organized by folks from the community helping their neighbors—such as the Soul Patrol, a Seventh Ward neighborhood relief and rebuilding effort led by longtime community leader Dyan French, known to locals as Mama D—and from nonofficial noncorporate relief networks like Common Ground Relief and the Rainbow Family. One of the grassroots relief workers who had been around from the beginning said to me, "The so-called first responders were neither. They didn't get here first, and they weren't responsive."

disaster tourists

"I want as many people to come visit here as possible," one Lower Ninth Ward resident told me as we walked past the infamous breached levees and destroyed homes of his neighborhood. "The national media has forgotten us; the politicians in DC have forgotten us. I support anything to get the word out." Among the people of New Orleans, this sentiment is common—that the country has moved on, and if people were to come here and see, maybe they would bring attention and consciousness.

Beginning days after the storm, New Orleans hosted a stream of celebrities and political players, from Sean Penn to a United Nations human rights envoy to a series of public relations visits from President Bush. Women of the Storm, a nonpartisan group led mostly by wealthy white women from New Orleans, raised a lot of cash and publicity for their mission to fly to Washington and convince congressional representatives to come and view the devastation.

Driving through the Lower Ninth Ward, even a year after the storm, you still see scattered groups on guided or unguided tours—residents surveying their homes, tourist-filled buses and vans filled with church volunteers, scruffy activists on bikes. People come to see the levee and to view the general devastation (still very much present).

"It was frustrating and painful at first," former mayoral candidate and Lower Ninth Ward resident Greta Gladney told me, referring to the people that have come to view her neighborhood.

> Before December 2005, in order to see our own neighborhood, we had to ride on a tour bus, while contractors, insurance adjusters, journalists, and police and soldiers could walk around there as much as they wanted. Politicians were using our neighborhood for leverage, to get more money from the federal government. But they don't want the Lower Nine to be rebuilt, so the money they get from our suffering is not going to come to us.

Many people have come through New Orleans promising to bring our stories out. But what does all of this witnessing add up to? "The story of what's happening here is not something you can just jump into," said local filmmaker Royce Osborn. "Things have changed, big and small; unless you were aware of what the city was like beforehand, you may not be able to convey that." When others tell New Orleans' story, they bring their own filters and analysis. Without the context of the structures of racism, corruption, and neglect that caused the devastation, it becomes just another act of God.

the resources

When I saw the floodwaters rising in New Orleans, I feared poor people would be cut out of the reconstruction money. What has surprised me is the extent to which the entire city has been left out. Though some local elites have profited, on a deeper level—from levees to housing aid to business loans—the money necessary to rebuild New Orleans simply never came.

Even progressive resources have been scarce. Left and liberal foundations and nonprofits have already spent tens of millions of dollars earmarked for the Gulf region. But according to recent studies, most of that money did not go to New Orleans-initiated projects, and, in fact, much of it went to the same East and West Coast nonprofits who have traditionally received the majority of grants—organizations with more experience in writing funding proposals and pleasing the funding networks.

New Orleans and the South in general have a long history of outsiders spending large sums of money for organizing without community leadership or involvement. Such efforts almost always fail. See, for example, the AFL-CIO's infamous "HOTROC" campaign in the late 1990s, in which millions of dollars were spent over several years and countless organizers were sent to New Orleans with the aim of organizing the city's tourist industry. In the end, there were virtually no successes to point to. Without community input, these efforts are usually misdirected from the start. Meanwhile, vital local efforts go unfunded and unsupported.

A wide array of grassroots people of color led organizations—most of them in existence since before Katrina—have organized tens of thousands of New Orleanians in the struggle for a community-led relief, reconstruction, and return, with very little attention from funders or media.

For example, INCITE! has brought delegations of women of color organizers from around the US to support its Women's Health and Justice Initiative, to start a women's health clinic and resource center. Advocates for Environmental Human Rights has worked with community organizations to bring a human rights framework and analysis to the grassroots struggle and has also actively taken part in these struggles—by, for example, bringing local community members to the United Nations to present testimony about the US government's human rights violations in New Orleans. The African American Leadership Project has organized community forums that have brought messages from the grassroots level to the mayor and city council. The People's Hurricane Relief Fund and the People's Organizing Committee have brought in large numbers of volunteers—mostly youth of color—to engage in direct organizing.

Latino Health Outreach Project (LHOP) is another example of a local organization functioning without outside support. LHOP began as a project of the Common Ground Health Clinic in the weeks after the storm to provide Latino day laborers with medical care. Clinics were set up wherever the laborers congregated—at hotels and campsites where they were staying and even at a restaurant on Canal Street where many of them would hang out on Friday nights. Combining health care and partnership with local grassroots organizers—a partnership in which the organization takes leadership from and is accountable to local people of color led organizations—LHOP has provided one of the best examples of what an alternative to corporate relief could look like, as well as a model of a partnership between local leadership and out-of-town volunteers.

These organizations have challenged not only the priorities of the elite in the reconstruction of our city, but the foundations and structure of corporate reconstruction and profiteering. The assumptions and systems they are challenging are at the heart of our nation's gross inequalities.

criminalization

Another vital local organization is Safe Streets/Strong Communities, a grassroots coalition of groups seeking to reform New Orleans' criminal justice system. Perhaps nothing better illustrates the cruelty of the militarized relief we saw in New Orleans than the treatment of incarcerated New Orleanians pre- and post-Katrina, and especially the situation of the prisoners who were in Orleans Parish Prison at the time of the storm.

When Hurricane Katrina hit, there was no evacuation plan for the 7,000 prisoners in the New Orleans city jail, generally known as Orleans Parish Prison (OPP), or the 1,500 prisoners in nearby jails. According to firsthand accounts gathered by advocates, prisoners were abandoned in their cells while the water was rising around them. They were subjected to a heavily armed "rescue" by state prison guards that involved beatings, mace, and being left in the sun with no water or food for several days, followed by a transfer to maximum-security state prisons.

Ursula Price, a staff investigator for the indigent defense organization A Fighting Chance and a member of the Safe Streets/Strong Communities coalition, met with several thousand hurricane survivors who were imprisoned at the time of the storm. The stories she heard were chilling: "I grew up in small-town Mississippi. We had the Klan marching down our main street, but I've never seen anything like this."

In March 2006, Safe Streets/Strong Communities released a report based on interviews with more than 100 prisoners who had been locked up since pre-Katrina. It found that the average number of days people had been locked up without a trial was 385. One person had been locked up for 1,289 days. None of them had been convicted of any crime. "I've been working in the system for a while," Price said. "I do capital cases, and I've seen the worst that the criminal justice system has to offer. But even I am shocked that there has been so much disregard for the value of these people's lives."

Samuel Nicholas was imprisoned in OPP on a misdemeanor charge and was due to be released August 31, two days after the storm hit. Instead, after a harrowing journey of several months, he was released February 1, 2006. He still shudders when he thinks of those days in OPP:

> We heard boats leaving, and one of the guys said, 'Hey man, all the deputies gone.' We took it upon ourselves to try to survive. They left us in the gym for two days with nothing. Some of those guys stayed in a cell four or five days. People were hollering, 'Get me out. I don't want to drown. I don't want to die.' We were locked in with no ventilation, no water, nothing to eat. It's just the grace of god that a lot of us survived.

Benny Hitchens was incarcerated for unpaid parking tickets. "They put us in a gym, about 200 of us, and they gave us three trash bags, two for defecation and one for urination. That was all we had for 200 people for two days."

"We have a system that was broken before Katrina," Price observed, "that was then torn apart, and is waiting to be rebuilt."

"This ain't just started; it's been going on," Nicholas added. "I want to talk about it, but at the same time it hurts to talk about it...It's not the judge, it's not the lawyers, it's the criminal justice system. Everybody who goes to jail isn't guilty. You got guys who were drunk in public, treated like they committed murder."

After the hurricane, the rounding up and incarceration of suspected "looters" was the first city function to restart. Due process and civil liberties were almost nonexistent for new arrestees, who were put in cages in a makeshift prison at a Greyhound bus station, with no access to phones or lawyers.

"Despite all of the horror we are seeing daily, my hope is this is an opportunity for change," Price told me. "OPP corruption is being laid bare. People being held past their time is nothing new in this system; it's just more extreme now. This is something to organize around and fight against." In the months since its founding, Safe Streets/Strong Communities has done just that, combining a grassroots organizing strategy—working directly with the incarcerated, the formerly incarcerated, and their family members—with political pressure and legal support. In its first months, the group has already succeeded in radically transforming the city's indigent defense board from a corrupt and negligent home for cronyism to a body staffed with criminal justice-reform advocates. At the same time the group has been able to mobilize a large grassroots base and become a force in city and state government.

the volunteers

Among progressive and radical communities around the country, perhaps the mostly widely known post-Katrina relief organization is Common Ground Relief. The Common Ground Collective was formed in the days after the disaster. It was an atmosphere in which the discussion among politicians and the media had moved from one of concern for storm victims, to violent hatred.

"Three hundred of the Arkansas National Guard have landed in the city of New Orleans," said Louisiana governor Kathleen Babineaux Blanco at a press conference on Friday, September 2, sounding almost hungry for bloodshed. "These troops are fresh back from Iraq, well trained, experienced, battle tested and under my orders to restore order in the streets. They have M-16s and they are locked and loaded. These troops know how to shoot and kill and they are more than willing to do so if necessary and I expect they will." Graffiti appeared all over the city reading, "You loot, we shoot." In white neighborhoods, armed gangs began patrolling the streets. To this day, we still don't know how many innocent black folks were killed for being in the wrong place at the wrong time.

In this racially charged moment, former Black Panther and New Orleans native Malik Rahim's first call was for white allies to come to stand between black community members and white vigilantes. His call went out widely, and soon Rahim's house became a campsite for mostly white, mostly young, mostly anarchist volunteers. As word continued to spread, more volunteers arrived, with supplies, a lot of energy, and a wide array of skills. Soon Rahim had arranged for his neighborhood mosque to be transformed into a free community health clinic. Other volunteers set up a wireless internet zone, a solar powered shower, and more projects every day.

Within a few weeks, the newly formed Common Ground Relief had a distribution network reaching 16,000 people in the New Orleans area and had set up a free health clinic serving hundreds of people. Many had not seen a doctor in years or even decades. In November, the group issued a mass call for volunteers that brought in 300 mostly young and white activists the week of Thanksgiving and hundreds more in the weeks that followed.

By the summer of 2006, the group had attracted thousands of volunteers, most of them sleeping on floors in recently reclaimed and cleaned buildings with makeshift electricity and sometimes without running water. The group—anchored by a core of organizers and coordinators that had been living in New Orleans for almost a year—had gutted hundreds of houses, started a newspaper and radio station, reopened at least one school, and established a number of other initiatives, including bioremediation projects, a community garden, and a wetlands restoration project.

The global justice movement added this disaster to a global revolutionary tourism circuit that travels from the Jenin refugee camp in Palestine to occupied factories in Argentina and Zapatista communities in Chiapas. Many of these new arrivals live and socialize in the Ninth Ward's Bywater neighborhood. The Bywater was already gentrifying pre-Katrina, but with the influence of Common Ground, that process seems to have accelerated. Many in the local organizing community remain suspicious of these outside volunteers, and the racial naïveté that many of them brought has hardly helped.

"We are talking about doing trainings; we are asking some groups down here who specialize in this to help train volunteers about their white supremacy. Some of them are taking it and some are not. Some are running around acting like slave masters," Curtis Muhammad, a New Orleans-based organizer and cofounder of the People's Organizing Committee and the People's Hurricane Relief Fund, told writer Walidah Imarisha in a widely circulated article. "White people are going to have to learn to obey and follow directions," Muhammad continued. "They can help us, feed us, house us, but we are not the slaves. They can't lead us."

"Activists gain a certain credibility by coming here," adds organizer Bridget Lehane, discussing the analysis of the People's Institute for Survival and Beyond, a New Orleans-based anti-racist training organization. "They can go home and talk about what they've seen and done here, in this historic moment and place, and it gives them a status, but what are they leaving behind?"

I've lived in New Orleans for only a few more years than the newly arrived Common Ground Relief volunteers. In many ways, the issues they have faced are ones that I have grappled with since I moved here, as a white activist attempting to be in solidarity with and accountable to a community that I am divided from by privilege. My hope is that the crowds of people coming through will take their stories home and revitalize our movements.

Many volunteers no doubt have learned nothing from being here. However, many have learned a great deal, and the experience has affected their worldview. One year from now, and five years and ten years from now, the people who have come through New Orleans in this difficult and challenging and intense and beautiful time will be active in their own communities. The leadership in coming struggles—the people doing exciting organizing and activism and resistance—will have gained vital inspiration and energy from this unique and incredible and horrible historic moment.

"Activists are changing the framework from 'I want to help' to seeing New Orleans as a key stronghold of resistance to injustices of this country," explained Chris Crass, an organizer with the Oakland-based antiracist Catalyst Project, who came to New Orleans last summer to support antiracist organizing among volunteers. "The challenge is to keep witnessing, to keep doing the relief work, but also to put in political education as a vital part of all of this. Then to take that knowledge, that experience, back to people's homes, to spread it around the US."

the fight in the neighborhoods

The organizations mentioned above are just one facet of New Orleans' resistance on the ground. There are also traditional community groups such as Social Aid and Pleasure Clubs, mutual aid institutions founded in the black community during the Reconstruction era that continue to this day. And throughout the city, there is a deep history of civil rights organizing.

Organized resistance rose up spontaneously wherever New Orleanians found themselves, including in hotels, shelters, and trailer parks. In spring 2006, I visited Renaissance Village, an evacuee community of more than 500 trailers located north of Baton Rouge on land owned by a youth prison. Residents I spoke to were aching to come home. "Last year I was a middle-income American, a homeowner—I never imagined I'd come to this," said Hillary Moore Jr., a former city employee exiled in a small trailer in the middle of the complex. Living alone, Moore barely fits in his trailer—it's so small. When he spoke about a family of five living next door, I couldn't imagine how they could possibly all squeeze in.

Displaced from their own neighborhoods, residents were attempting to form new community in the camp, but faced many obstacles. High among them is the stress and the pressures of living in such close and uncomfortable conditions. "Living here, you meet people under unusual circumstances," Moore explained politely.

Not long after moving in, Moore and others organized a residents' council, with an elected board and open meetings every week. "We got tired of a lot of things Keta [the contractor company managing the park] was doing and we decided to organize because we realized there is strength in numbers," he told me.

Another dramatic example of grassroots community response can be seen in the rise in prominence and influence of New Orleans' neighborhood associations. These organizations—most of which existed pre-Katrina but have seen membership numbers and involvement multiply since—

have become important as places for politicians, architects and designers, planners, and foundations and other funders to go to for input and to lend support.

The rise in prominence of these neighborhood associations represents a real possibility for direct democracy and community involvement. They have had successes—in designing their own plans for rebuilding, in resisting the destruction of their neighborhoods, in fighting a landfill near residences in New Orleans East, in getting trash pickup started, and much more. However, with so much of the city still displaced, the membership of these organizations is biased toward those who have returned or who never left, which, in turn, reflects the racist and classist nature of this disaster. For example, even neighborhoods in which the majority of the residents are African American, such as Gentilly and Broadmoor, have been represented by neighborhood associations in which the majority of the members—in my observation—are white.

As the planning process has continued, these issues have risen to the forefront. The reconstruction of New Orleans, if it happens, will take several years and billions of dollars. The question of who will make the decisions in that process remain unanswered.

the battle of new orleans

As of this writing, nearly a year after Katrina, New Orleanians are still dispersed around the US. Most have had limited or no access to their homes and feel that the city and developers are deliberately attempting to keep them out. "If that's the plan, then it's backfiring," Tanya Harris, a Lower Ninth Ward resident told the *New York Times* in December 2005. "I'm not seeing that laid-back New Orleans character right now. I'm seeing a fighting spirit. I mean, my grandmother would chain herself to that property before she allowed the city to take it."

Every time I see a family moving back, I am inspired by this small act of resistance and courage, this dedication to community. Every day, I see little acts of resistance, in second lines and other cultural expressions. I see people going to what seems like the thousandth neighborhood planning meeting. I see people demonstrating in the streets. I see people being kind and generous in the face of the cruelty of the city's elite who tried to keep them out. I see people giving their neighbors places to stay and food and always being ready with a friendly greeting.

This has been a sad time for anyone from New Orleans, or anyone that cares about the people of the city. It has been a time of increased drinking, suicide, and depression. But it has also been a beautiful and inspiring time. The people of New Orleans are standing up and fighting back in a historic struggle for justice, joined by progressive allies from around the world and reinforced by a tradition and culture of resistance. This culture of resistance continues to inspire those of us seeking to rebuild New Orleans with a community vision. It has sustained me when it seems hopeless. In the end, it may be the best hope we have.

---

endnotes

1   Cornel West, interview by Joanna Walters, *Tikkun Magazine Online*, September 2005, http://files.tikkun.org/current/article.php?story=20061028140331323.

Unless stated otherwise, all quotes referenced in this chapter are from direct conversations and interviews conducted by the author. Portions of this chapter were originally published in the magazines *Left Turn* and *ColorLines*.

the obscurity of black suffering
jared sexton

No imagination is required to see this scene as a direct remnant of slavery.

—William Grier and Price Cobbs, *Black Rage*

I can think of no better way to begin a meditation on the theme of this anthology—"what lies beneath"—than with reference to Tavis Smiley, the premier black media personality of the early 21st century. Smiley, as many know, is spearheading the recent "Covenant with Black America" (CWBA) campaign, "a national plan of action to address the primary concerns of African Americans today," and whose capstone publication of the same name quickly reached the number-one spot on the vaunted *New York Times* best-seller list in the spring of 2006.[2] The text, which compiles ten topical essays from noted experts, was edited by Smiley with blessings from Children's Defense Fund founder Marian Wright Edelman and publishing assistance from the well-known and independent Third World Press. In the promotional abstract for this broad-based, if modest, program for reform in education, policing, health care, employment, housing, etcetera, the editor offers the following admonishment: "African Americans continue to face devastating disparities on nearly every level. However, the time has come for African Americans to shift the conversation from talking about our *pain* to talking about our *plan*." One should immediately wonder, of course, why we cannot do both, why, that is, talking about pain must be de-emphasized or muted, put aside or substituted, before talking about plans can commence. What is this shift meant to signal, we might ask, if not a change in direction or perhaps attitude? Is this new shift not another mode of defense against the malicious accusation of our incurable (or *inconsolable*) shiftlessness?

The sentiment of timely expediency proffered by the CWBA—a solemn promise to "stop talking and start doing" based on a belief that "actions speak louder than words"—plays to an understandably popular urgency that emanates quite directly from the rigors of everyday survival faced by the vast majority of black people in the United States and, not incidentally, from the continued material precariousness and acute status anxiety of the black middle class. However, I submit that, in point of fact, "we who are dark"[3] have done precious little talking about our pain in this post–civil rights era and probably a bit too much posturing about our plans. If anything, we have a surplus of plans, many of them quite sound and longstanding and unrealized. What we do not have is a language, much less a political culture, that adequately addresses the complexity of our position(s), our predicament(s), and our pain(s) without recourse to euphemism. As a result, we are perhaps more inarticulate about our pain today—in the age of transnationalism and multiracialism—than we have been at any other historical juncture. I mention "pain" here, but it is better to speak more precisely of "suffering" and to do so in the fullest sense of the word: indicating not only pain, which everyone experiences, all oppressed people, at least, but also that which we must bear—*uniquely* and *singularly*—that which we must stand and stand *alone*.

I should say at the outset that I am not reporting on Hurricane Katrina and its aftermath in this light. Rather, I am commenting on what I have encountered of the extant reporting, both mainstream and independent, on Katrina. This essay presents a second-order reflection on how various media outlets, public officials, policy analysts, social critics, and service providers have covered the unfolding of the disaster; how they have evaluated the ways the disaster has or has not been attended by various relief/recovery/reconstruction efforts; and, finally, the historic significance they attribute to the disaster itself.

That being said, we should review the basics.

Hurricane Katrina was the most destructive and most expensive "natural disaster" in US history. It impacted an area of 140,000 square miles—nearly the size of Iraq—and government expenditures to address the damage have surpassed $100 billion, a price tag that is predicted to exceed $200 billion. If the death toll reaches the projected maximum of 3,500 (a number that surpasses the nearly 3,000 killed on September 11, 2001), Katrina will also be the country's deadliest, surpassing the 1928 Okeechobee Hurricane, which claimed some 2,500 lives in southern Florida. The hurricane and attendant flooding produced more than 1.3 million internally displaced people, most of whom remain dispersed across hundreds of cities in all 50 states, the District of Columbia, and Puerto Rico.[4] Tens of thousands of those dispersed by the storm will likely be displaced for a second or third time in the near future as the Federal Emergency Management Agency (FEMA) discontinues its long-term housing and utilities voucher program.[5]

Since the landfall of Hurricane Katrina on August 29, 2005, national and international attention on the matter has ebbed and flowed, punctuated by phase changes in its wake from relief to recovery to reconstruction. Discussions immediately polarized into debates, with participants tending to bifurcate into two broad camps: on the one hand, a conservative-reactionary camp that would excuse the government response, claiming that there was, in fact, no disproportionate impact on the black poor or that the storm's effects were simply unforeseen and that those who were left behind simply chose their fates, including the paramilitary police repression provoked by their supposed criminality; on the other hand, a liberal-progressive camp that would levy accusations and provide criticism of government neglect, incompetence, or malfeasance. The latter position, despite the range of its manifestations, has been preemptively codified in official accounts by the release of the report of the Senate Committee on Homeland Security and Governmental Affairs entitled *Hurricane Katrina: A Nation Still Unprepared.*[6]

Left critique emanating from alternative media outlets has, on balance, remained the loyal opposition, differing in degree but not in kind from such mainstream conclusions, revealing little beyond that which has already been captured, with far greater circulation, by the embarrassed and sorrowful musings about "structural" inequalities of race and class offered in the *New York Times*, *Washington Post*, or *Chicago Tribune*. There we find a consistent refrain: Hurricane Katrina should serve not simply as the proverbial wake-up call for the disaster relief apparatus or as a plea for better coordination across various levels of government, but also as an indictment of tragically persistent social divisions generally attributed to the residual effects of Jim Crow, the excesses of the "Reagan Revolution," or the draconian domestic costs of neoliberal corporate globalization. In this way, the black victims of Katrina are represented as a conglomerate stand-in—a sign or symptom—for larger political and economic processes: the infamy of the current administration, the shame of a nation, or the scandal of the present regime of accumulation. They are, as legal scholar Lani Guinier would have it, "the canary in the mine."[7]

Strange, then, that black people in this scenario could serve as both minor indicators of much larger problems and, at the very same time, as that presence that eclipses or overshadows the plight of what are generically referred to as Katrina's "other victims": those groups supposed to be forgotten in the national imagination, those rendered invisible or unknown by the media spotlight on the plight of blacks, those whose stories remain untold. In response, reporting surfaced within days—initially from various ethnic media outlets and eventually from the corporate media as well—that focused on the fate of Asians (Chinese, Filipinos, Koreans, Vietnamese), Latinos (Hondurans, Mexicans), American Indians (Chitimacha, Choctaw, Tunica-Biloxi), and poor whites along the Gulf Coast. Other venues reported with great concern and no less prominently on the fate of commercial livestock and the welfare of various "companion species"[8] such as domesticated cats and dogs. To cite just two examples, the February 10, 2006, report by KPFT, 90.1 FM, the Pacifica affiliate in Houston (the city receiving perhaps the single largest influx of human evacuees) was titled "Katrina: The Forgotten Victims"; the *Journal of the American Veterinary Medical Association* featured the October 15, 2005, headline "Katrina's Other Victims."

It would not be difficult to demonstrate how this multiracial (and multispecies) reframing participates in the larger—and deeply convoluted—attempt to displace the so-called black-white binary in discussions of race in the US. It is claimed therein that this transcendence of the black-white binary is necessary in order to, as it were, broaden and complicate our view of things, to address a more complex ("brown" or "beige") reality. Needless to say, this position implies that discussions to this point—discussions of black suffering—have been narrow, simple, and plain.[9] Yet, nothing could be further from the truth. Not only because the matter of black suffering is infinitely complex, as is the history of struggle within and against it (a complexity that is pulverized by the presumption bandied about so often today that "we already know about blacks"). But also, perhaps more important, because black suffering—especially in its gendered and sexual variations—is in no way visible, known, remembered, or properly told.[10] It was not, as so many have maintained, "exposed to global view" or "put on center stage" in the days and weeks and months following Katrina's landfall. In fact, as the recent work of writer and filmmaker Frank Wilderson III demonstrates compellingly, such exposure is structurally foreclosed by the force of antiblackness.[11] This foreclosure is especially clear in the case of those who ostensibly wanted so much to remark upon the spectacle of black suffering. Those struck by the proliferation of images of black victims "reduced to an animal-like state"[12] found themselves, nonetheless, calling the nation to task for "turning a blind eye" toward or "living in denial" about a nondescript and wide-ranging *poverty*.

It is as if there is no way to talk about antiblackness, or the matrix of racial slavery, without reducing it to those anemic empirical markers that pass for class analysis in the US.[13] It is as if the only way to register this *ongoing* event of racial slavery is to analogize it to neocolonial subjugation (for example, from the Persian Gulf to the Gulf of Mexico) or assimilate it to processes of economic exploitation.[14] Yet, as Mike Davis observes:

> As a result [of the disaster], not just the Black working class, but also the Black professional and business middle classes are now facing economic extinction while Washington dawdles. Tens of thousands of blue-collar white, Asian and Latino residents of afflicted Gulf communities also face de facto expulsion from the region, but *only the removal of African-Americans is actually being advocated as policy.*[15] [emphasis added]

Concurrent with this mass removal, federally sponsored programs promoting the "Latinization" (and "lightening") of the post-Katrina workforce seek to remake Orleans Parish in the likeness of Los Angeles County (a metropolitan area in which blacks make up less than 10 percent of the local population, compared with 45 percent of Chicanos/Latinos).[16] I want to stress that this does not mean that immigrant laborers from Mexico or Central America are driving these changes—quite the contrary. They are subject to the devastating macroeconomic effects wrought for more than a decade by pernicious free-trade agreements (e.g., NAFTA, DR-CAFTA), and they are then exploited ruthlessly, without even minimal protections, by private contractors upon their arrival in the US.[17] But this does not mean that they are, therefore, outside the sphere of complicity, however unwitting—or desperate—we judge it to be.[18]

Preceding and prefiguring in important ways the considerable upsurge in the immigrant rights movement as of late,[19] this immense population transfer is especially telling given the myriad warnings issued about the imminence of a Katrina-style disaster and the state's so-called failure to plan accordingly. In retrospect, it appears that the state and corporate interests were planning all too well, looking forward to capitalizing on a moment of predatory opportunity. The foreknowledge of impending destruction—not only its general likelihood but also its *particulars*—was obscenely old, dating back, at least, to the landfall of Hurricane Betsy in 1965.[20] This is so much the case that it is entirely unreasonable to call the position taken up by various state agencies a "failure," an "unduly delayed response," official "negligence," or even government "malfeasance." It is unreasonable, in fact, to call it anything but *expectancy*: waiting for the execution of a disaster that was not only predicted, but whose probability was also actively produced by the consistent reconfiguration of Jim Crow segregation and urban ghettoizing and refined by decades of aggressive public policy. It was, in a word, *engineered*: the Hurricane Ivan false alarm evacuation in September 2004 fully previewed the catastrophe of late summer 2005, serving as a sort of morbid dress rehearsal.[21]

Evidence of this bipartisan premeditation—and this wishful thinking—is only capped by the post-disaster maneuvering of the power elite to restructure New Orleans in the gentrified image of a most lucrative and racially hygienic collective fantasy. As the Associated Press noted, "Hurricane Katrina [may] prove to be the biggest, most brutal urban-renewal project Black America has ever seen,"[22] a project buttressed by an array of exclusions—from bureaucratic disenfranchisement to the denial of relief aid and social services to the permanently forestalled right of return—and enforced by the further militarization of public space, armed to the teeth and grinning from ear to ear. And yet, as community activist and political journalist Jordan Flaherty writes from ground zero in New Orleans:

> On a deeper level, the very idea of "Hurricane Katrina Relief" [and eventually reconstruction as well] encourages the idea that the problem is just the damage from the hurricane, and that if we can get people back to where they were pre-hurricane, everything will be OK. The status quo pre-hurricane was, and is, the problem.[23]

In this light, we can see clearly that the overwhelming impact of Hurricane Katrina could not have been prevented; the disaster could not have been averted. That is, at least not within the framework of our present theoretical and practical labors. Fortunately, alternative approaches to the aftermath of the disaster have emerged from the political imagination of grassroots activists and organizers in the region, an imagination firmly rooted in the black radical tradition. The deep historical sensibility and the expansive vision of transformation that animate such local initiatives have been aptly portrayed by Eric Mann in his book, *Katrina's Legacy: White Racism and Black Reconstruction in New Orleans and the Gulf Coast.*[24] There, Mann is able to generate a multidimensional analysis of the wreckage produced by the deluge without diminishing the *centrality* of black liberation struggle to any notion of adequate redress for *all* those affected.

In order to situate the event of Hurricane Katrina squarely within the afterlife of slavery, Mann discusses the prospect of a radical redevelopment plan under the heading of a Third Reconstruction, one drawing upon the dynamic arc of the first (1865–1877) and second (1955–1975) historic iterations. If, he argues, the modern civil rights and black liberation movements sought to refashion the postbellum project anatomized so brilliantly by DuBois,[25] then perhaps this early-21st century effort, spreading out along the pathways of dispersal from the epicenter of the crisis, may yet reignite the best of those "two decades of the sixties" that shook US society—and the global system it continues to dominate—to its foundation. In truth, we must aim at undoing, in the present, an epochal association that predates this country's founding moments. Beyond, or perhaps before, overturning the prevailing relations between people *and* property, we must address those unthinkable processes that continue to render people *as* property.

endnotes

1   An earlier version of this essay was presented at Williams College on April 29, 2006, at the symposium "Policing the Black Body." Thanks to Professor Joy James for the generous invitation and for the labor of organizing the event. Thanks also to Professors Jafari Allen, Ted Gordon, Kara Lynch, Gina Ulysse, João Vargas,

jared sexton

and Frank Wilderson III for their active participation at that gathering.

2   Tavis Smiley, ed., *The Covenant with Black America* (Chicago: Third World Press, 2006). In fact, *The Covenant with Black America* is the first nonfiction book published by a black-owned press to top the list. See Sherrell Wheeler Stewart, "'The Covenant' Tops Bestseller List—the First for a Black-Owned Publisher," *BlackAmericaWeb. com*, April 18, 2006, http://www.blackamericaweb.com/site.aspx/bawnews/covenant418. It is important to note as well that these impressive sales figures are driven by a largely black readership, despite the dry, policy-based language that characterizes its various essays. See DeWayne Wickman, "A Black 'Covenant' Draws Wealth of Readers," *USA Today*, March 27, 2006, http://www.usatoday.com/news/opinion/columnist/wickham/2006-03-27-wickham_x.htm. In my view, the popularity of the book and the full-house attendance at each stop of its eight-city promotional tour has less to do with the insights or the analysis or the merits of the platform advanced therein than with the more general obfuscations of the contemporary political milieu. For additional information on the CWBA, see the official Web site: http://www.covenantwithblackamerica.com.

3   The phrase is taken from the title of Tommie Shelby's *We Who Are Dark: The Philosophical Foundations of Black Solidarity* (Cambridge, MA: Harvard University Press, 2005). He, in turn, draws the phrase from a passage in W.E.B. DuBois's famous essay "Criteria of Negro Art." The eponymous epigraph reads as follows:

> What do we want? What is the thing we are after? As it was phrased last night it had a certain truth: We want to be Americans, full-fledged Americans, with all the rights of other American citizens. But is that all? Do we want simply to be Americans? Once in a while through all of us there flashes some clairvoyance, some clear idea, of what America really is. We who are dark can see America in a way that white Americans cannot. And seeing our country thus, are we satisfied with its present goals and ideals?

4   Matthew Ericson, Archie Tse, and Jodi Wilgoren, "Storm and Crisis: Katrina's Diaspora," *New York Times*, October 2, 2005, http://www.nytimes.com/imagepages/2005/10/02/national/nationalspecial/20051002diaspora_graphic.htm.

5 Shaila Dewan, "Evacuees Find Housing Grants Will End Soon," *New York Times*, April 27, 2006, http://www.nytimes.com/2006/04/27/us/27vouchers.html?ex=1161748800&en=623234ab69aeda97&ei=5070.

6 Senate Committee on Homeland Security and Governmental Affairs, *Hurricane Katrina: A Nation Still Unprepared*, http://hsgac.senate.gov/index.cfm?Fuseaction=Links.Katrina.

7 Lynne Duke and Teresa Wiltz, "A Nation's Castaways," *Washington Post*, September 4, 2005, http://www.washingtonpost.com/wp-dyn/content/article/2005/09/03/AR2005090301548.html. Guinier's use of this popular phrase is an allusion to her recent book, coauthored with Gerald Torres. Lani Guinier and Gerald Torres, *The Miner's Canary: Enlisting Race, Resisting Power, Transforming Democracy* (Cambridge, MA: Harvard University Press, 2003).

8 Donna Haraway, *The Companion Species Manifesto: Dogs, People, and Significant Otherness* (Chicago: Prickly Paradigm Press, 2003).

9 The literature on the function of "the black-white binary paradigm of race" in the United States is too vast to summarize adequately. However, we can note preliminarily that it involves a broad dissatisfaction with the framing of US racial discourse primarily or exclusively in terms of the historical oppression of blacks by whites. Typically, it is claimed that such framing excludes critical attention to the histories of nonwhite people of color, including especially the politics of immigration and multiracialism. For examples of the standard critique of the binary, see Richard Delgado and Jean Stefancic, eds., *The Latina/o Condition: A Critical Reader* (New York: New York University Press, 1998) and Frank Wu, *Yellow: Race in America Beyond Black and White* (New York: Basic, 2002). There are, at least, two fundamental problems with this critique. First, it often serves to *expunge* critical discussions of black history altogether—either by omission or by spurious analogizing between the position of blacks and those of other people of color—rather than *expand* the discourse as it supposedly claims to do. Second, it relies upon an insidious notion of black empowerment vis-à-vis other oppressed groups to make its claims about the exclusion of nonblack people of color by *both* whites *and* blacks. It thereby rationalizes the aforementioned expunging. For a trenchant rebuttal of the standard critique, see Sora Han, "The Politics of Race in Asian American Jurisprudence," *UCLA Asian Pacific American Law Journal* 11, no. 1 (2006); Mari Matsuda, "Beyond, and Not Beyond, Black and White," in *Crossroads, Directions, and New Critical Race Theory*, ed. Francisco Valdes, Jerome McCristal Culp, and Angela Harris (Philadelphia: Temple University Press, 2002); and Jared

Sexton, "Racial Profiling and the Societies of Control," in *Warfare in the Homeland: Incarceration in the United States*, ed. Joy James (Durham, NC: Duke University Press, forthcoming). I suspect that these problems are structural rather than a series of oversights. That is to say, they are endemic to the grounding assumptions of the critique, namely that racial formation in the post–civil rights era United States is organized by a color line between whites and nonwhites. However, as Kasinitz argues, "For the children of nonblack, nonwhite immigrants … it is important to remember that race is mutable and the color line may be moving. The central cleavage in American life was once clearly between whites and nonwhites. Today there is some evidence that it is between blacks and nonblacks." Philip Kasinitz, "Race, Assimilation, and 'Second Generations,' Past and Present," in *Not Just Black and White: Historical and Contemporary Perspectives on Immigration, Race, and Ethnicity in the United States*, ed. Nancy Foner and George Fredrickson (New York: Russell Sage Foundation, 2004), 288. His findings regarding the "black-nonblack divide" are consonant with a growing number of prominent scholars in the humanities and social sciences. See, for instance, Charles Gallagher, "Racial Redistricting: Expanding the Boundaries of Whiteness," in *The Politics of Multiracialism: Challenging Racial Thinking*, ed. Heather Dalmage (Albany, NY: SUNY Press, 2004); Herbert Gans, "The Possibility of a New Racial Hierarchy in the 21st Century United States," in *Rethinking the Color Line: Readings in Race and Ethnicity*, ed. Charles Gallagher (New York: McGraw-Hill, 2003); Lewis Gordon, *Her Majesty's Other Children: Sketches of Racism from a Neocolonial Age* (New York: Rowman & Littlefield, 1997); George Yancey, *Who Is White? Asians, Latinos, and the New Black/Nonblack Divide* (Boulder, CO: Lynn Reiner, 1997).

10 Saidiya Hartman, *Scenes of Subjection: Terror, Slavery, and Self-Making in 19th Century America* (New York: Oxford University Press, 1997)

11 Frank Wilderson III, *Incognegro: From Black Power to Apartheid and Back* (Boston: Beacon Press, 2007).

12 Lynne Duke and Teresa Wiltz, "A Nation's Castaways," *Washington Post*, September 4, 2005, http://www.washingtonpost.com/wp-dyn/content/article/2005/09/03/AR2005090301548.html.

13 For an extended example of this anodyne form of class analysis, see *New York Times, Class Matters* (New York: Times Books, 2005). For a more robust treatment of class in the United States that amends the *Times* anthology, see John Bellamy Foster, "Aspects of Class in

the United States: An Introduction," *Monthly Review*, July–August 2006, http://www.monthlyreview.org/0706jbf.htm, and the entire issue of the *Monthly Review* in which this article is published.

14 "As the 21st century starts, the idea of a colorless struggle for human progress is unfortunately back with a vengeance … What is distressingly new is the extent to which indictments of antiracism, and even attacks on the use of race as a concept, come now from liberalism and from the left." David Roediger, "The Retreat from Race and Class," *Monthly Review*, July–August 2006, http://www.monthlyreview.org/0706roediger.htm.

15 Mike Davis, "Gentrifying Disaster," *Mother Jones*, October 25, 2005, http://www.motherjones.com/commentary/columns/2005/10/gentrifying_disaster.html.

16 Gregory Rodriguez, "La Nueva Orleans," *Los Angeles Times*, September 25, 2005, page M1.

17 Rukmini Callimachi, "Illegal Workers Face Hardship in Big Easy," *Washington Post*, June 6, 2006, http://www.washingtonpost.com/wp-dyn/content/article/2006/06/07/AR2006060700376_pf.html.

18 I am instructed on this point by Gayatri Spivak, who writes that those disavowing the trajectory of "eurocentric economic migration (and eventually even political exile)" can only persist "in the hope of justice under capitalism." Thanks to Sora Han for drawing my attention to this important passage. Gayatri Spivak, *A Critique of Postcolonial Reason: Toward a History of the Vanishing Present* (Cambridge, MA: Harvard University Press, 1999), 396. Sora Han, "The Politics of Race in Asian American Jurisprudence," *UCLA Asian Pacific American Law Journal* 11, no. 1 (2006): 2.

19 Brian Kwoba, "Birth of a *New* New Left? The Immigrant Rights Movement," *Counterpunch*, May 12, 2006, http://www.counterpunch.org/kwoba05112006.html.

20 "Washing Away: A Special Report" (five-part series), *Times-Picayune*, June 23–27, 2006, http://www.nola.com/washingaway/.

21 Mike Davis, "Poor, Black, and Left Behind," *Mother Jones*, September 24, 2004, http://www.motherjones.com/news/update/2004/09/09_414.html.

22 Mike Davis, "Gentrifying Disaster," *Mother Jones*, October 25, 2005, http://www.motherjones.com/commentary/columns/2005/10/gentrifying_disaster.html.

23 Jordan Flaherty, "Race, Relief and Reconstruction." *Left Turn*, October 6, 2005, http://www.leftturn.org/Articles/Viewer.aspx?id=702&type=w.

24 Eric Mann, *Katrina's Legacy: White Racism and Black Reconstruction in New Orleans and the Gulf Coast* (Los Angeles: Frontlines Press, 2006)

25 W.E.B. DuBois, *Black Reconstruction in America, 1860–1880* (New York: Free Press, 1998).

other sources include

Bourne, Joel. "Gone with the Water." *National Geographic.* October 2004. http://www.nationalgeographic.com/ngm/0410/feature5.

Dyson, Michael Eric. "Did Hurricane Katrina Reveal a Historic Reality?" in *Come Hell or High Water: Hurricane Katrina and the Color of Disaster.* New York: Basic Civitas, 2006. This essay is also available online at http://www.msnbc.msn.com/id/10995079.

Grier, William, and Price Cobbs. *Black Rage.* New York: Basic Books, 1992.

the meaning of "disaster"
under the dominance of white life
dylan rodríguez

Hurricane Katrina is being invoked as an exceptional episode in US history—as something already framed in the past tense. However, the living time of Hurricane Katrina, which I understand here as an ongoing material history of rigorously organized, state-facilitated, and militarized white racial dominion—in this instance focused on, though not limited to, the eviscerated urban geography of New Orleans and the Lower Ninth Ward—presents an acute opportunity to express and firmly restate the logic of dominance that encompasses our collective existence. The racial and racist violence that continues to unfold through this alleged natural disaster—a violence often apocalyptic in its form and staging—attests to the conspicuous normalcy of white supremacy to the everyday historical functioning of the United States.

The United States of America is *inhabited and reproduced* by a white supremacist animus—an everyday mode of existence that permeates both hegemonic institutions and ordinary people—that has largely manufactured Katrina, fabricated its structure of inevitability ("God has allowed it," according to white Christian nationalist leader Billy Graham[2]), enabled and ensured its maximum deployment as a protogenocidal "tragedy," and celebrated it as an opportunity for nationalist (urban) renewal, framed in the language of a mourning racial sentimentality.[3]

We risk serious political error and moral bad faith if we conceptualize this "disaster" outside of its crystallization of the complex social meanings of American white civil existence—a form of collective life that is disingenuously universalized to the point of transparency, such that the very assertion of a categorical "white life" smacks insult to common cultural and intellectual sensibilities. Hurricane Katrina has abruptly displaced the "multicultural" pretensions of the American post–civil rights national and global formation and reinserted the *sanctity* of white existence, white bodies, and white life as the central condition of the nation's coherence. Katrina thus speaks to the essential structuring techniques of white life as a system of dominance.

My purpose in this essay is to offer a situated reflection on how the time of Katrina articulates a global indictment of white life, framed by the possibility of a political and existential identification with the context and substance of a critical common sense of black and third world death. This common sense, shared especially by black and indigenous people across historical moments in the conquest and racial formation of the United States, elaborates the fundamental and aggressive violence of white existence. The time of Katrina thus bespeaks the relevance of black subjection in the United States to the *global* conceptualization of racial dominance, colonial and neocolonial power, and state violence in the shadow of disaster.

the social truth of "black refugees"

While accountings of indigenous, Latino/a, Asian, and poor white suffering at the hands of Katrina continue to be written, we ought to be clear that the fundamental economic, cultural, and state/military logic governing the discrete geographic and human drowning of a post-segregation, though effectively apartheid, New Orleans is animated by the sturdy symbiosis between black disposability and American nation building. This is to say that contemporary black social death[4] is characterized by the seemingly instantaneous social alienation of a delineated category of racially pathologized people whose formal status within the civic body is permanently marked by the irreconcilable—and socially defining—tension between centuries of racially formed, genocidal enslavement and the multiple historical *recodifications* of black subjection to institutionalized white supremacist violence in the nominal (and relatively recent) historical aftermath of racial chattel slavery (in fact, enslavement and involuntary servitude were recodified in 1865 as a "punishment for crime whereof the party shall have been duly convicted"). The crucial contradiction that surfaces in the living moment of Katrina's wake, in other words, is not limited to the stubborn and almost trite disjuncture between aspirations toward fully enfranchised (hence state-protected) African "American" civil existence and persistent antiblack state violence and racism. The more important and productive antagonism is embedded in Hurricane Katrina's re-enshrinement of the specificity of American white supremacy—and, specifically, mass-based black bodily and geographic liquidation—*as an epochal articulation of democracy, state-building, and nationalist well-being.* Katrina, in other words, was good for (white) America.

The time of Katrina indicates the fundamental *irrevocability* of white life as a unilateral declaration of war: it is a life-or-death struggle to ascertain the collective white body's ascendancy over the mundane conditions of black suffering and constitutes a dynamic structuring of domination over the form, duration, and condition of "life" itself.

Black death and displacement, ordained through the ritualized negligence and organized dysfunctioning of the American state during and after the anticipated destruction of Katrina—a hurricane that, it cannot be overemphasized, was meteorologically well predicted—can and must be understood as the organized and enforced condition of contemporary liberal multiculturalism, the most current and recent innovation of white supremacy that feeds and fosters a desire to, in plain words, live as (we imagine) white people do. When located alongside coterminous structures of white supremacist, nationalist, and democratically articulated antiblack violence— for example, racially militarized policing and the post-1970s prison industrial complex—Hurricane Katrina is well within the historical conventions of American white civil society itself, amplifying and restoring the sanctity of white bodily integrity (and multicultural aspirations toward the same) through state-sanctioned and popularly consumed productions of black bodily disintegration. Katrina, in its presentation of black social liquidation as a *naturalized* state of emergency for an allegedly isolated population of black people, gratifies the multiculturalist desire to flee the condition of "blackness" toward the imagined sanctum of white life.

While we are living in the age of multiculturalist white supremacy, wherein "people of color" are increasingly, selectively, and hierarchically incorporated/empowered by the power structures—government, police, universities, corporations, etcetera—that have historically formed the institutional circuits of US apartheid and racist state violence, Katrina reminds us that white America occupies a category of social existence that is without global parallel. It lives within a historical structure of life wherein it is capable of *presuming entitlement* to things like bodily integrity, communal (read: racial) security, and militarized state responsiveness in a manner that no other human category can allege to share in this moment. Imagine, then, the sheer accumulation of racially organized death, vulnerability, and bodily disintegration that must accrue in order to render these white life entitlements so massively that they can, in fact, be taken for granted by whites *and* their racial others.

As others in this collection more adequately elaborate, the sanctity of white civil existence continuously resonates through the time of Katrina, fostering a material—and thoroughly theatrical—conceptualization of black life that affirms the alienated relation between the material consequences of black racialization—for example, living in a place below sea level next to obsolete levees that await instantaneous collapse—and the *nationalist* postulation and posturing around black civil existence, a mythological modality of social being that is produced through the constant evidencing of its basic fraudulence. It is precisely the national *disposability* of black life and well-being that makes the concept of the black ("African American") citizen so *in*dispensable to the contemporary American project. Therefore, we must consider that the popular rhetoric positing the crisis of Katrina's "(black) refugees" actually bespeaks the *white supremacist social truth* of the United States, rather than a stubborn racist refusal to incorporate and assimilate black subjects, lives, and bodies into the vernacular realms of American humanism or "citizenship." From there, we are collectively obligated to confront white American existence with at least a minimal, political agenda: to radically and decisively undo its premises of social and philosophical coherence, overwhelm it with global displacements of its asserted and presumptive dominion over the lived meanings of race/place/body, and thoroughly demystify the massive (and massively tolerated) architecture of violence that constitutes the normative peace and entitlement of white life itself. After all, what is "peace," really, in the time of Katrina et al?

Katrina especially amplifies how the historical production of a white supremacist racial existence has been continuously fortified through an institutionalized immunity of white bodies from categorical (that is, racial) fragility—white bodies are generally alienated from and systemically *unfamiliar with* forms of collective, unexpected bodily violence and premature death. In this sense, the relation of "disaster" to white life is that of a *socially reproductive* technology: the social, political, and physical liquidation of the white world's durable racial antagonist(s) reproduces the transparent universality—the very "normalcy"—of white civil existence and bodily integrity and provides a material opportunity for white life to quite literally *transcend death.*

identifications with/and black common sense

A reflection on political and philosophical positioning is appropriate here. I arrive at this reflection on Hurricane Katrina through my own Pinoy (or "Filipino") genealogy, as someone born and raised in the US while sustaining lifelong affective, extended familial, and imaginary connections to another place. For reasons I'm not sure I can fully understand or explain, Katrina resonates with me in ways that render sympathy and mourning as inappropriate, even offensive reactions to what has happened and continues to happen. In my gut, I do not feel as if Hurricane Katrina was/is a "tragedy," and I find myself viscerally objecting to its being characterized as such. While there are innumerable tragedies—personal and political—composing the mosaic of this historical moment, Katrina strikes me as something closer to a planned atrocity, and the spectacle of its becoming sits with me as a scene of white popular enjoyment,[5] wherein the purging/drowning of black people provided an opportunity for white Americana to revel in its entitlement to remain relatively indifferent to this nearby theater of breathtaking devastation. (The racial dramatization of Katrina also reminds that the pleasure of charity is significantly derived from the sense that one is extending assistance to others despite the absence of any absolute moral or material obligation to do so.) The white world was, in one important sense, wallowing *and* rejoicing in its utter unfamiliarity with what it was watching in the last days of August 2005. Hence the time of Katrina is, and can only be, a living history in which white subjectivity is both spectator and architect. This structure of witnessing and orchestration, perhaps, is what most disorients my own sensibilities.

The 1991 explosion of Mt. Pinatubo in the Philippines (the second-largest volcanic eruption in the 20th century), which is arguably best known for having effectively destroyed the massive Clark and Subic Bay US military bases, is prominent in Filipino diasporic consciousness and historical memory. While the context, geography, and sociopolitical impact of the Pinatubo eruption do not conveniently parallel, or sustain easy comparison with, the atrocity that is the focus of this book, the explosion undoubtedly contributed to the atmospheric and environmental conditions of possibility for Hurricane Katrina. The ash, gas, and toxins distributed by the volcano were so significant that they effectively reduced the overall temperature of the earth by 1.5° Celsius, altered global wind circulation, and destroyed a significant portion of the planet's ozone layer.[6] Beyond these mind-numbing environmental consequences, and the 800 killed and 200,000 displaced by the eruption and subsequent lahars, Mt. Pinatubo is perhaps most significant to the Filipino diaspora for its signification of instant mortality and involuntary, unexpected "evacuation" at the hands of God (or, if you like, diasporic susceptibility to an inaccessible transcendental agency). This lasting significance is undoubtedly enhanced by the fact that Mt. Pinatubo is less than 60 miles away from metro Manila, the center of Philippine civic life. In the decade after Pinatubo's explosion, the Clark and Subic Bay military bases were nominally shut down as operational sites of US occupation and were, more accurately, resurfaced as sites for the facilitated influx of neoliberal capital, renovated as places of tourist enjoyment in fulfillment of a white militarist nostalgia, and periodically re-operationalized for US militarization after 2001.[7] (We can only anticipate that things similar will happen in New Orleans and the Gulf Coast during the coming decade.)

At the time of the Pinatubo explosion, I clearly recall feeling that disaster and social upheaval were the modus operandi of that/my other place. In my short lifetime (I was 17 when the volcano erupted) the Philippines had come to represent a geography of political terror and commonly witnessed mortality. The first exposed corpses I ever saw and truly remembered (outside the controlled environment of the funeral home or church) were inscribed in the endlessly broadcast images of assassinated Marcos opposition leader Ninoy Aquino—photos and video captures of his mutilated face and bloody barong (a Philippine men's shirt worn on formal occasions) were widely circulated in the weeks following his death—and the more visceral memory of a nameless man whose body I observed being retrieved from the water a day after he had drowned near a Philippine beach, near my grandparents' house. What I have seen, heard, and read of the time of Katrina is already condensing in my historical memory as something uncomfortably similar to this kind of extrapolated and extended trauma—that is, a refraction of death that seems to be telling me something essential about the place where I live, move, and come into/from.

Unexpected displacement and premature death are absolutely unremarkable to Filipinos, above and beyond exposure to the worst of naturalized environmental disaster (although I will not recite the socioeconomic, health, or mortality data here). Whether it is due to the reified status of the Philippines as the most underdeveloped and structurally impoverished country in the Asia Pacific or its colonial and neocolonial subjection to US hegemony and American-proctored, hypermilitarized domestic state violence, the scene of Katrina is, in some important (though perhaps underexamined) ways, not altogether alien to us. Members of the Filipino diaspora, across class and regional distinctions, can almost universally state that they are immediately connected to the fallout from environmental hazard/disaster, assassination, acute government repression, or US military occupation/mobilization. Mt. Pinatubo's devastation, however, also reveals that this diasporic connectedness is neither seamless nor unmarked by its own reinscriptions of localized productions of racialized hierarchy and dominance. Rarely invoked in remembrances, commemorations, and (re)narrations of the eruption is the fact that "hardest hit among the casualties were the Negritos who were not immunized from diseases and even shunned the treatment of doctors."[8]

The national/racial positioning of the Negrito peoples reflects the Spanish colonial and Euro-American anthropological etymology of their naming, and the Negrito ethno-racial categorization serves as a convenient categorical incorporation of a much broader collection of indigenous Philippine groups, including the Aetas (or Aytas), who inhabited the immediate region of Mt. Pinatubo. The colonial, anthropological, and contemporary Philippine national/racial imaginary conceptualizes the Negritos through a version of "epidermalized"[9] blackness that articulates with notions of an aboriginal (and quaint) Philippine "tribal" premodern. As historically racialized, and conventionally racially pathologized subjects, Aetas self-consciously rupture universalizing notions of Philippine nationalist, diasporic, "racial," and (pan)ethnic identity. In the Aeta/Negrito vernacular, there is a clear delineation between indigenous/Aetas/Negritos and "straight hair"/lowlander Filipinos. Two Aetas who survived the eruption thus consider the delineation of (racial) difference in the moment of disaster. Victor Villa writes:

> I believe that Aytas and straight-hairs have certain similarities in thinking and certain differences in behavior. Aytas are just as intelligent as straight-hairs; the only difference is our lack of education. We eat differently, we dress differently. Straight-hairs like wearing shoes and fancy clothes, while Aytas are comfortable with *bahags* (loin cloths).

> The lowlanders look down on Aytas. They even sneer at us as if we were direct descendants of monkeys.[10]

Elvie Devillena echoes Villa's thoughts in her own reflections:

> When people see that you are short, they already know you are an Ayta. They can tell you are Ita by your skin, height, or speech pattern … No matter how you look, if you are an Ayta, it will always show. People have called me "Ayta, Ayta, Ayta. Kinky hair, kinky hair, kinky hair." They say that with so much derision. Sometimes we are called *beluga* because we have dark skin. People from Manila think that Zambalas is filled with wild, savage Ayta people.[11]

The Aeta people's embodiment and dense signification of Philippine racial formation is further refracted in one state official's account of the Pinatubo relief efforts.

> Tarlac governor Mariano Un Ocampo narrated how he was both amazed and amused at the Aetas' refusal to eat the canned goods given to them. "They have no taste at all for the canned goods," he said.

> About the only exception is the pork and beans in cans, Ocampo added. "But they would wash away the sauce and just eat the beans."

> Slow to adapt themselves to situations … this attitude also contributed to the many deaths among them, particularly children …

> But Ocampo expressed admiration for their integrity and honesty. "They would return to us the

extra relief items given to them," he said, recalling occasions when the Aetas brought back the excess in the number of tents distributed to them for their shelter.

"I would never expect our straight-haired people to do that," he said.[12] [emphasis added]

Such a discourse echoes the categorical status of the Negritos as opportune material for anthropological and ethnographic knowledge production during the latter part of the 20th century. According to German anthropologist Stefan Seitz, writing in 2004, "The Aeta form part of the Philippines' aboriginal population, the so-called *'Negritos.'* Negritos differ from other Filipino groups in their racial phenotype, characterized by curly hair, dark complexion and small stature and by their lifestyle with its strong focus on foraging strategies."[13]

Seitz continues by remarking on the emergence of scholarly interest in "hunter-gatherer studies" during the 1960s, and the particular anthropological fixation on "secluded, 'pristine' cultures with as many 'archaic' traits as possible." He contextualizes the current location of the Aeta people in the anthropological imaginary by considering the acceleration of ethnographic studies in the 1970s and 1980s, asserting that "as a result of this renewed interest, the Negritos of northeastern Luzon joined the San of southern Africa and the Pygmies of central Africa as the hunter-gatherer societies most intensely studied by anthropologists."[14] In fact, Villa's and Devillena's self-narrations of Aeta difference, read alongside Ocampo's paternalism and Seitz's academic rendition of Aeta/Negrito phenotype, constitute differently positioned reinscriptions of the vague, though still overdetermined, cultural and anthropological/"racial" distinctions that distinguish particular Philippine ethnic and aboriginal populations and geographies from those of commonly identified (and nationally authenticated) "Filipinos."

The Aeta/Negrito condition—and its "official" representation through state and academic discourse—in this moment of Philippine national crisis compels a rereading of Mt. Pinatubo's eruption and a reconsideration of how this moment might alter our understanding of the larger genealogy of Filipino familiarity with disaster, *especially in relation to the naturalized global linkages between "blackness" (Negritoness), social liquidation, racial subjection, and historical obsolescence (aboriginalness).*

A central political and theoretical problem defining the global and historical structure of Filipino intimacy with death and terror is its relative alienation from a common sense of white supremacy that *sees, analyzes, and viscerally experiences* mortal Filipino suffering as the logical global and historical condition of white (American) life. It is white civil existence and its analogues (including elitist versions of Philippine cosmopolitanism and diaspora), in other words, that create and circulate the "racial" and aboriginal existence of the Negrito people and their global cohorts and install them as the durable centers of gravity for precisely the forms of civil, social, and biological death rendered so immediately visible in the US through the racial apocalypse of Hurricane Katrina. Such a racial common sense is precisely what black people in the United States have involuntarily obtained, and rigorously, commonly theorized, over the past several centuries of national formation.

This critical black common sense—the notion, consistently sustained as a Fanonist "historical truth,"[15] that black peoples' intimacy with death and terror is the *fundamental purpose of white civil existence, and, perhaps, global white life itself*—is (again) being stunningly vindicated as plans are made to "reconstruct" New Orleans as a gentrified white metropolis.[16] Perhaps it is the latent possibility of manifesting an authentically global and translocal significance to this racial common sense that most resonates with me.

The time of Katrina amplifies the necessity for a political articulation of white supremacy that is "radical" in the most historically contextualized sense of the term. We can understand the planning of Katrina in its geographic and political specificity as antiblack state violence and orchestrated, "natural" population control, while also situating it in relation to the global material structuring, and material genealogy, of white Americana as a perpetual state of warfare that is fundamentally *racial* in its historical architecture, social vision, and militarized ordering of human disposability. I am suggesting that the gravity of black death and displacement in the living aftermath of Katrina creates a radical possibility for black common sense to resonate with, and provide substantial political-theoretical premises for, other (neo)colonized, underdeveloped, and racially pathologized peoples' *self-conceptualizations and global political identifications* in relation to things like (US and US proctored) state violence, "natural" disaster, poverty, disease, and bodily disintegration. Perhaps most important, this suggests the global rather than narrowly "national" or even "regional" significance of US-based antiblack violence as a modality of white supremacist social ordering: naturalized American antiblackness can be considered as a material foundation on which other circuits of global dominance—including neocolonialism, nationalism, "globalization" and "empire"—rely for matrices of war making, racial subjection, and hierarchized material and ideological structures of human mortality.

Thus, Mt. Pinatubo's eruption did not merely contribute to the global climatic condition for Katrina, it also reveals the deep connection between apparently disparate "natural" occurrences which, in turn, surface as linked formations of global white supremacy and racism, the latter of which Ruth Wilson Gilmore conceptualizes as "the state sanctioned and/or extralegal production and exploitation of group-differentiated vulnerabilities to premature death."[17] Aeta testimonials in the aftermath of the Pinatubo eruption suggest a firsthand, organic accounting of the Philippine state that more clearly renders its relation to the American white supremacist/racist state. While most Philippine journalistic, state, "relief aid," and academic commentary on the post-eruption condition of the Aeta people patronizingly fixates on their "irrational" refusal to accept medical aid, laments their naive hesitance to pursue (or eagerly welcome) government assistance, and references the

Aetas' quaint adherence to spiritual and "animistic," rather than pragmatic, conceptualizations of life and survival, there persist among the Aeta traces of precisely the critical common sense that formulates a fundamental *dis*identification with the social and political logic of the Philippine national/racial formation and invokes latent possibilities for a rearticulation of cosmology, history, and identity that can exist alongside the critical black common sense of the Katrina moment. A sampling of Aeta thought in the wake of Pinatubo:

> I think all these [events] happened because God is testing us.

> According to the elders, they have always taken care of Pinatubo. The word *pinatubo* in our language means "nurtured with care." Since long ago, our ancestors have taken care of the mountain. But, perhaps in time, our leaders' minds had been tainted with a destructive nature. Thus, they allowed the Philippine National Oil Company, which had no right to disturb the mountain, to get in ... Since it was the government that ordered the operation, the Aytas couldn't do anything about it.[18]

> We wanted the government to know that the Philippine National Oil Company [PNOC] promised our people many good things, like schools and employment for the Aytas. Many of us liked the idea. But not everyone thought it wise to drill into Pinatubo. The Ayta leaders thought that these operations would affect our way of living, the environment, the water, and our resources ...We didn't want PNOC to endanger these basic needs. But we were betrayed ...That was when Pinatubo started to emit smoke. It was around April.[19]

"We were provided with multicolored plastic tents for shelter. We were told that they were the best possible solution to our problem," said Nestor Solomon. However, the Aeta added, "We know that tents are hardly suitable for the summer or the rainy season. It was hardly a home. It never gave us warmth ... Whenever the sun shines, it becomes unbearably hot inside a tent. When it rains, it becomes too cold for comfort because the ground gets damp ... For many months, we had to endure sleeping close to the cold and damp earth," he added. Comparing his life before and during the Pinatubo eruption, he said, "I always slept well up in the mountain."[20]

> Many died at the evacuation center at Cabalan. It's so painful that many were claimed by diseases like measles, diarrhea, bronchopneumonia ... Every day, from June to July, August, September, people died. The fact that many Aytas in Cabalan died makes me cry. There were a lot of medicines, but most were useless, like paracetamol. There were also hospitals, like the two converted rooms in the school, but people died anyway. This is the sad plight of the Aytas.[21]

> The relief operations weren't any better either. The sardines were old and already expired ... Many died in Cabalan because of flies. The flies were on our food, in our coffee. These flies caused diarrhea.

> And the sardines—the cans were rusted inside. That is why I did not eat sardines. I showed them to Mrs. Gordon [wife of Kakilingan mayor Dick Gordon] and I asked her why we got expired sardines. All she said was, "Just throw it away, Son." So I did. And when I did, the cans exploded. I found out that the sardines were over five years old.[22]

> When we relocated to Iram, the government constructed the road. However, the bridge they built was weak, and it gave way during Typhoon Kadiang. ...In Iram, the Department of Environment and Natural Resources allotted 70 hectares for our farm lots and 30 hectares for our home lots. But it's already 1994, and we still haven't received our farm lots. That's why a lot of Aytas still don't have a decent means of livelihood.[23]

> An Ayta without land is a fish out of water. Bring him to the city and he will wither away. Government projects do not address this very important issue

> We need funds for land. The government gives us funds for electricity and facilities. They give us roads,

schools, hospitals, and comfort rooms. But what they don't give us are the means to feed ourselves. A home without anything to eat is worthless ...

The government is not solving anything. Many Aytas are now becoming domestic workers, cowhands, and beggars. If the government acted quickly after the eruption, this would not have happened.[24]

This brief series of reflections from displaced Aetas implicates a fundamental structure of *planned social obsolescence*[25]— "We native Aytas feel that our culture is slowly being erased as we become more civilized"[26]—as well as semipermanent subjection to "client" status under the hegemonic Philippine state. It also provides the basis for elaborating a deeper set of political, cultural, and philosophical linkages between differently located "black"/indigenous peoples, woven through politically constitutive scenes of disaster. By way of brief example: the Aeta reflection on the Philippine neoliberal state's tampering with the ecology of the mountain resonates with the common, long-standing suspicion shared among black Louisianans (and many others) that the US state was largely responsible for *manufacturing and (urban) planning* the human casualties of Katrina (for example, through decades of refusal to address the obsolescence of levees "protecting" the Lower Ninth Ward, its creation of a veritable police state across different "black refugee" sites, and its generalized withholding of response/relief capacities at the pinnacle of the hurricane's force).

My reflection on Mt. Pinatubo here is intended to amplify the moment of Katrina, rather than displace or dilute the gravity that Katrina brings to discussions of black life, survival, struggle, and liberation. I am suggesting that movements, activists, and intellectuals inhabiting *different* genealogies and heritages of subjection to white supremacist violence are called upon, in such moments of racial apocalypse, to accelerate their different modalities of struggle against global white civil existence and its conditions of possibility. Such moments foreground the potential for a global *political* resonance of critical black common sense that forms at least one philosophical and pragmatic basis for rewriting history, in the sense of both scholarly vocation and living, radical praxis. If the structuring dominance of white life is to be displaced or obliterated, and the cultural-material possibility of an authentic human existence somehow vindicated, then those whose death and displacement is *taken for granted* truly encompass a state of emergency for the white world. Natural disaster, as a modality of human elimination, coercive "modernization" (in the case of the Aetas), strategic urban population control (in the case of black New Orleans), and racist state violence is simultaneously a radical *narrative* moment in the elaboration of global hierarchies of life and death and a radical *political* moment for comprehending the productive necessity of massive, collective, progressive transformative struggle against white civil existence, which watches in tragic delight as disaster renders new opportunities for expanding white life's spheres of dominion and domination.

For many Filipinos across the global diaspora, the explosion of Mt. Pinatubo may always in some sense allegorize humility before the hand of God, but it can also be re-narrated as a moment of profound intimacy with the mortal logic of living for a century under white Americanist dominion: What does it mean for one's kin to live at the base of an active volcano, nearby two active US military bases? What of the Aeta/Negrito sensibility that posits fundamental suspicion with Philippine state and civil attempts to offer (and, in places, coerce) "relief" from their disfranchisement, displacement, and exposure to preventable illness? If some form of war, evacuation, human disaster, and collective death are "built in" as the virtual inevitability of such a (racial) geography, then how should Filipinos (in and beyond the United States) understand themselves in relation to black people in the time of Katrina?

Strident and open Filipino negrophobic racism notwithstanding, it may well be that the only possibility for serious *political* kinship between blacks and Pinoys (locally and diasporically, beyond liberal, culturalist, or compensatory Filipino negrophilia) exists in the space of proximity and familiarity that can only be shared as we approach our differently produced— though somehow still stubbornly *common*—identifications with the horror of a collective vulnerability to sudden mortality and bodily subjection to higher forces (whether "God," "nature," the US state, or officially sanctioned white supremacist violence). What if we understood the death and destruction resulting from Mt. Pinatubo's eruption, and the genealogy of Filipino suffering and disaster itself, as mutually and materially *articulating with* black death and displacement before, during, and beyond the time of Katrina? The statement issued a year after Mt. Pinatubo's eruption by the Central Luzon Ayta Association, part of a Philippine umbrella network of indigenous peoples' organizations, complexly echoes and differently locates a black critical common sense of the state in moments of disaster.

> One Year Has Passed. Slowly and Swiftly.
>
> Slowly. The promises were slowly fulfilled. Medicines and food were slowly delivered. Rescue slowly reached us.
>
> Swiftly children and elders got sick. Death was swiftly running after us. We were soon forgotten, and our problems quickly passed from one government agency to another.[27]

I am not pleading for another modality of multicultural coalition or even black-Pinoy solidarity here. Instead, I am asking for a different paradigm of *identification*—encompassing the realms of spirituality, cosmology, (racial) identity, cultural imagination, and political dreaming/fantasizing—one that precedes (and I hope generates) a different kind of praxis, across the localized sites of US white supremacy.

I am also openly wondering if this autobiographical reflection is really an extended articulation of a particular political desire, to instigate and participate in a radically collective global communion of people who are capable of mustering the voice to (at least) accuse the white world of conspiring and reveling in the death of others. It is in the act of making such an accusation that we might see the genesis of political labors that push and break the limits of rationalistic, formulaic, and pragmatist agendas challenging American hegemony and neoliberal capital. Of course, such an accumulation of identification and bonding, alongside others, could well contribute to the end of white life as we know it.

conclusion: empire, evil, humanism

Of our contemporary global ordering, Michael Hardt and Antonio Negri write in their widely read text *Empire*:

> Empire is emerging today as the center that supports the globalization of productive networks and casts its widely inclusive net to try to envelop all power relations within its world order—and yet at the same time it deploys a powerful police function against the new barbarians and the rebellious slaves who threaten its order. The power of Empire appears to be subordinated to the fluctuations of local power dynamics and to the shifting, partial juridical orderings that attempt, but never fully succeed, to lead back to a state of normalcy in the name of the "exceptionality" of the administrative procedures.[28]

Surely there is a "juridical ordering" that shapes the actual administration of "disaster"—such is seen in the tendency to overfocus on the bureaucratic fumblings of FEMA in the case of Katrina. What I find more significant here, however, is the manner in which "natural" disaster itself, as a *normalization of profound bodily violence against "slaves and barbarians,"* most often escapes the critical lens of theorists, activists, and even human rights advocates. We need to demystify the notion of "natural disaster" as something that *naturally* kills the abject of Negri and Hardt's empire. The apparent unavoidability of things like volcanic eruptions and category 5 hurricanes must be theoretically and politically distinguished from the *proctored processes and architectures of mass-scale death* that are manufactured in the midst of natural disaster's presumed inevitability. Perhaps the targeted chaos, socially planned displacement, and flexible (non)administration of "relief" and fatality in moments of disaster illustrates the global dominion of white civic life as the fundamental collective project that simultaneously precedes, constitutes, and overdetermines empire, globalization, neoliberalism, etcetera.

What concerns me here is the kind of gravity that "barbarians and rebellious slaves" embody in the crafting of global white supremacy, a technology of violence and social architecture of dominance that somewhat dis-/relocates the machinery of Negri and Hardt's conceptualization of empire as "world order." Arguably, what manifests as amplified police power within the global operations of white supremacy—neocolonial rule, militarized occupation, perpetual domestic and global war—is the ongoing *condition of possibility* for empire itself. Unless there are *constant deployments of violence* that consolidate the capacity to *presume* the earthly integrity and transcendence (universality) of white life, the apparatus of empire—for example, its structure of governmentality, disciplined bodily mobility, and coercive orderings of local and global "peace"—would implode.

To be clear: the allegedly encompassing and globally integrating constitution of empire as an arrangement of power *does not* subsume, decenter, or supersede the apartheid and disintegrating logic of global/translocal white supremacy. The state violence that Hardt and Negri relegate to the realm of "police" power is actually much more than a state of exception to the "normalcy" of empire's arrangement of power. While their notion of world order usefully offers the notion that "Empire is born and shows itself as crisis," and suggests that mobilizations of police power speak to the embedded "contradictions" of empire—"the question of the definition of justice and peace will find no real resolution"—the time of Katrina suggests the existence of entire categories of people for whom the civic discourse of "justice and peace" is rendered *entirely irrelevant.*

This structured irrelevance may help explain why the racial apocalypse of Katrina brings forward eerie (and generally undertheorized) resonance between black American premature

death and third world mass suffering and normalized population liquidation. Unnatural black death, alongside indigenous
planned obsolescence, is constitutive of US nation building
across historical moments, while (undeclared) war, disaster,
and protogenocide (sometimes referenced as "overpopulation"),
is central to the global formation of contemporary white supremacy in the neocolonial and postcolonial worlds. Imagine,
then, the kind of governmental, administrative, cultural, and
(para)military labor required to expose a racially identifiable urban "civil"/"citizen" population to the front lines of *preventable*
mass displacement and death and to then successfully fortify
this exposure with multiple mobilizations of domestic police
forces that focus and contain the fallout of such a scene.

Finally, disaster, conceived in the presence of white supremacy, definitively and conclusively means the end of any
viable, much less rational, possibility for the future of white
liberal humanism. Something that many survivors of European
and Euro-American colonialism, slavery, and genocide share is a
durable belief in the existence of evil, a basic conception that its
force of possibility is always lurking in the overlapping spiritual
and material worlds, and a powerful (though often understated)
conviction that evil inhabits and possesses the white world, its
way of life, and its relationality to "others." Liberal white humanism, which constantly circulates and rearticulates notions of a
shared universal "human" character, while morbidly militarizing
against manifest human threats to the integrity of the coercively
universalized white body, cannot authentically survive the moment of Katrina. In fact, white humanism can only survive at all
if it is capable of (again) reconstructing its apparatus of meaning
to accommodate the materialization of white evil in the face of
black New Orleans. Perhaps, then, another question we might
visit is, What does Katrina tell us of evil? What happens if
we look up and evil is armed absence and militarized neglect,
intentional and institutional without a doubt, but materialized
through the white world's persistent festival of health, happiness,
and physical integrity in the face of such incredible suffering?

1 Significant portions of this chapter emerged from extended conversations with Vorris Nunley (University of California, Riverside), whose friendship, support, and bottomless intellectual generosity allowed me an opportunity to elaborate thoughts on white humanism, liberalism, and state violence. This essay also benefited enormously from the incisive insight and critical eye of Setsu Shigematsu (University of California, Riverside). I also wish to thank Joey Fox for inviting this contribution to the book, and for her extraordinary patience throughout the editorial process.

2 Invoking the biblical story of Job, Graham told *Newsweek* managing editor Jon Meacham, "The Devil might have had nothing to do with this; I don't know. But God has allowed it, and there is a purpose that we won't know maybe for years to come." See "Newsweek Interview: Rev. Billy Graham," *Newsweek*, March 12, 2006. Around the time of this interview, Graham's son Franklin preached to an audience of over 13,000 in the New Orleans Arena, "I don't believe the hurricane was God's judgment, but I believe it's an honest question ... People are quick to blame God, but you know there is a devil. The Bible says he's the liar. He's the one who wants to destroy each and every one of us." See Gwen Filosa, "Graham Brings a Message of Hope," *Times-Picayune*, March 12, 2006, Metro section.

3 White enjoyment of both mundane and spectacular black suffering is a historical staple of American national and racial formation and has been the subject of both critical black intellectual work and traditional academic investigation for over a century. Four works that particularly shaped the ideas in this part of the essay are Ida B. Wells-Barnett, *On Lynchings* (1892; repr., Amherst, NY: Humanity Books, 2002); Malcolm X, *The End of White World Supremacy: Four Speeches* (New York: Arcade Publishing, 1971); Stewart E. Tolnay and E. M. Beck, *A Festival of Violence: An Analysis of Southern Lynchings, 1882–1930* (Urbana and Chicago: University of Illinois Press, 1995); and Saidiya V. Hartman, *Scenes of Subjection: Terror, Slavery, and Self-Making in 19th America* (New York: Oxford University Press, 1997).

4 See Orlando Patterson's extended comparative anthropology of social death in his classic text *Slavery and Social Death: A Comparative Study* (Cambridge, MA: Harvard University Press, 1982). Here I have chosen to emphasize the specificity of the genealogy of a *racially articulated and juridicially encoded* social death in the history of US racial chattel slavery.

5　While hers is a discussion of white enjoyment of mundane and unspectacular moments of black subordination and antiblack violence under the dominance of racial chattel slavery, the fundamental insight of Saidiya V. Hartman's work *Scenes of Subjection* is wholly germane here: central to the affective, juridical, and psychic structures of slavery (and white supremacist dominion over the black body) is the essential and multivalenced *availability* of black suffering for the consumption and use of white subjects.

6　See Giovanni Rantucci, *Geological Disasters in the Philippines: The July 1990 Earthquake and the June 1991 Eruption of Mount Pinatubo* (Rome: Italian Ministry of Foreign Affairs, Directorate General for Development Cooperation, 1994), 107–108; Maria Cynthia Rose Banzon Bautista, ed., *In the Shadow of the Lingering Mt. Pinatubo Disaster* (Quezon City, Philippines: University of the Philippines, 1993); and Eddee R.H. Castro, "Global Effects," in *Pinatubo: The Eruption of the Century* (Quezon City, Philippines: Phoenix Publishing House, 1991), 78–83. For other useful references to the immediate context of the Mt. Pinatubo eruption, see Lee Davis, *Natural Disasters: From the Black Plague to the Eruption of Mt. Pinatubo* (New York: Facts on File, 1992); and *Report of the Task Force on the Damage Caused by the Eruption of Mt. Pinatubo and Proposed Rehabilitation/Restoration Measures* Asian Development Bank Agriculture Department, August 1991.

7　Vernadette V. Gonzalez (University of Hawaii) has written of this intersection between militarization, tourism, and war in the Philippines in the essays "Touring Military Masculinities: Sacrifice and Gratitude in Corregidor Island and Bataan," in *Gender and Militarism Across the Asia Pacific* ed. Setsu Shigematsu and Keith Camacho (unpublished manuscript), and "Military Bases, 'Royalty Trips' and Imperial Modernities: Gendered and Racialized Labor in the Postcolonial Philippines," (unpublished manuscript).

8　Castro, *Pinatubo: The Eruption of the Century*, 2.

9　Frantz Fanon's well-known meditation on "The Fact of Blackness" best articulates the notion of race as a formation of power that condenses at the sight of the racialized body, more specifically the overdetermined site of the epidermis. In one famous passage from this essay, he reflects on his experience with a white child on a public train, whose exclamation "Look, a Negro!" instantly invoked the alienation of the black body/subject from human history, displaced by a racist "historicity" of blackness:

> Then, assailed at various points, the corporeal schema crumbled, its place taken by a racial epidermal schema.

> In the train it was no longer a question of being aware
> of my body in the third person but in a triple person. In
> the train I was given not one but two, three places. I
> had already stopped being amused. It was not that I was
> finding febrile coordinates in the world. I existed triply:
> I occupied space. I moved toward the other ... and the
> evanescent other, hostile but not opaque, transparent,
> not there, disappeared. Nausea ... [all ellipses in the
> original]

Frantz Fanon, "The Fact of Blackness," in *Black Skin, White Masks* (New York: Grove Press, 1967), 112.

10 Victor Villa, "ADA Chairman's Personal History and Ayta Consciousness," in Hiromu Shimizu, *The Orphans of Pinatubo: The Ayta Struggle for Existence* (Manila: Solidaridad Publishing House, 2001), 263.

11 Elvie Devillena, "Activities of PINATUBO and Ayta Consciousness," in Shimizu, *The Orphans of Pinatubo*, 288.

12 Castro, *Pinatubo: The Eruption of the Century*, 109.

13 Stefan Seitz, *The Aeta at the Mt. Pinatubo, Philippines: A Minority Group Coping with Disaster* (Quezon City, Philippines: New Day Publishers, 2004), 1–2.

14 Seitz, *The Aeta at the Mt. Pinatubo*, 19–20.

15 Fanon writes of racist colonial domination that it is a constitution of "history" itself:

> The colonist makes history and he knows it. And because
> he refers constantly to the history of his metropolis, he
> plainly indicates that here he is the extension of this
> metropolis. The history he writes is therefore not the
> history of the country he is despoiling, but the history
> of his own nation's looting, raping, and starving to
> death. The immobility to which the colonized subject is
> condemned can be challenged only if he decides to put
> an end to the history of colonization and the history of
> despoliation in order to bring to life the history of the
> nation, the history of decolonization.

Frantz Fanon, *The Wretched of the Earth*, trans. Richard Philcox (1963; repr., New York: Grove Press, 2004), 15.

16 See Mike Davis, "Gentrifying Disaster: In New Orleans, Ethnic-Cleansing, GOP-Style," *Mother Jones*, October 25, 2005; Jesse Jackson, "Eased Out of the Big Easy," *Chicago Sun-Times*, October 4, 2005; Gary Younge, "Big Business Sees a Chance for Ethnic and Class Cleansing," *Guardian* (London), April 20, 2006;

Nadra Enzi, "Katrina: The Aftermath," *Atlanta Journal-Constitution*, September 15, 2005.

17 Ruth Wilson Gilmore, "Race and Globalization," in *Geographies of Global Change: Remapping the World*, ed. R. J. Johnston, Peter J. Taylor, and Michael J. Watts (Oxford: Blackwell Publishing, 2002), 261.

18 Bienvenido Capuno, "Historical Consciousness of the Aytas," in Shimizu, *The Orphans of Pinatubo*, 105.

19 Aurelio Lahut, "PNOC Triggered Eruption and the Hard Life in Iram Resettlement Site," in Shimizu, *The Orphans of Pinatubo*, 142.

20 Barbara Mae Dacanay, *Mt. Pinatubo 500 Years After* (Quezon City, Philippines: Mass Media, 1991), 72–73.

21 Victor Villa, "Suffering Caused by the Eruption and Memories of Old Days," in Shimizu, *The Orphans of Pinatubo*, 152.

22 Emelito Melicia, "A Man Went Back to Higala Near Kakilingan," in Shimizu, *The Orphans of Pinatubo*, 181.

23 Victor Villa, "ADA Chairman," 262.

24 Ric Guiao, "Organization and Activities of CLAA for Sociopolitical Empowerment," in Shimizu, *The Orphans of Pinatubo*, 310.

25 This notion is concisely and brilliantly elaborated by native Hawai'ian scholar-activist Haunani-Kay Trask in "The New World Order," in *From a Native Daughter: Colonialism and Sovereignty in Hawai'i* (Monroe, ME: Common Courage Press, 1993), 79–84.

26 Jerry Cabalic, "Eruption and Ayta Consciousness," in Shimizu, *The Orphans of Pinatubo*, 216.

27 Statement of the Central Luzon Ayta Association, June 15, 1992, in Shimizu, *The Orphans of Pinatubo*, 36.

28 Michael Hardt and Antonio Negri, *Empire* (Cambridge, MA: Harvard University Press, 2000), 20.

political literacy and voice
joy james

for Kara

We do not believe that the American people who have encouraged such scenes by their indifference will read unmoved these accounts of brutality, injustice and oppression. We do not believe that the moral conscience of the nation—that which is highest and best among us—will always remain silent in face of such outrages.
  —Ida B. Wells, "Mob Rule in New Orleans," 1900[1]

read three images

A *Monthly Review* photograph of a tank with armed soldiers—actually members of the State Police Tactical Unit who with their assault weapons pointed down or slightly up just look like armed soldiers—patrolling the streets of New Orleans while black residents outside a shelter of "last resort" call out for help.[2]

A Reuters photograph of uniformed white men disciplining black men sprawled face down on dry concrete; the white men patting down and surveying the black men, who've been stopped in their efforts to flee catastrophe (marked as carjackers?); one officer positioning a foot inside the door of the postal vehicle he has just rescued. The caption reads: "Texas game wardens watch over people who were caught using a mail truck to try to escape New Orleans. They were freed but forced to continue on foot."

The image of a white couple wading through water with groceries juxtaposed with the image of a young black man wading through water with groceries—their respective captions identifying the white couple as "searching" for food and the black man "looting" for his.

speak three words: shoot to kill

Redundant death or overkill is mapped onto black New Orleans so strongly that most are silenced or speak feeble responses to the realities of institutional abandonment, neglect, paternal contempt and caretaking, and state and social violence before and after Katrina landed. Witness those who walk in and through a city turned urban graveyard—first moving and floating, then drying in mire—struggling to gain a foothold, and to voice a literacy that counters denials and executioners' commands levied against those "left to die." (Survivors wrote on a chalkboard in St. Mary's middle school, where they sought refuge from the waters flooding the Ninth Ward, "They left us here to die.") Challenging silence on the state's responsibility for death and social instability, *What Lies Beneath: Katrina, Race, and the State of the Nation* creates space for vocal, politically literate voices.

The images and language of post–Katrina New Orleans, like that of post–9/11 United States, inspire new voices, such as those presented in this anthology, and an infusion of radicalism into common sense or everyday politics to promote literacy relevant to crises where deadly domestic and foreign policies increasingly intersect (a quarter of the Louisiana National Guard was absent from relief efforts due to deployment in Iraq, where over 600,000 Iraqis, according to a Johns Hopkins study, and approximately 3,000 US citizens have died since the US invasion). This volume provides us with a grammar book shaped by previous battles for justice, love, and safety for self and community. The voices represented here, whether native New Orleanians or not, build a foundation to resist dehumanization, and so as part of the "voices of Katrina," echo historical narratives that frame and shape the meanings of current trauma, dislocation, and death.

litany for survival

Months before I traveled to New Orleans, searching for a "litany for survival," I reached for Ida B. Wells's writings on lynching and police brutality, assigning "Mob Rule in New Orleans" to my students as a grammar book on antiblack racism and social and state violence. Vilifying and policing, containing and punishing black bodies seemed more important to state officials than saving black lives in the days and weeks during which state officials and media sought to interpret and assign blame for human loss and man-made or compounded disaster following Katrina. That the state placed abandoned survivors under a shoot-to-kill edict to criminalize their right to survival left some of us momentarily speechless, and required more political literacy and critical voice than that readily available through the language of conventional politics.

As Governor Kathleen Babineaux Blanco and President George W. Bush drew a bulls-eye target around largely black survivors we had witnessed trying to survive—and some failing and so dying—without assistance from a state to which they swore some allegiance or belonging ("we're American, too"), words drew me and destabilized me until I realized that I had to translate my disgust and distress into political literacy. It was not human suffering per se, but suffering accompanied by repression embedded in the injunction of death for the resourceful who didn't want to roll or rot in misery that radicalized me into seeking more voice.

Literacy transports us into politics. Not always coherent or seamless, radical literacy is at least alive to possibilities for change and social transformation, possibilities for resistance. Resistance may start in crisis. If you reach a point where the state, by its own rhetoric, promises to use lethal force against responsible people who are trying to prevent their children, themselves, or others from prematurely dying or needlessly suffering, then you're at a crossroads. Here, the moment of crisis is compounded by the government, so that it seems logical to suggest, given the "shoot-to-kill" decrees, that good or competent (black) parents and community-minded survivors secure bulletproof vests before seeking ("looting") bottled water, baby formula, and pampers; or before taking vehicles to flee danger; or, having been stripped of technology at gunpoint by game wardens from an adjoining state, before attempting to cross bridges on foot into surrounding parishes—only to be turned away at gunpoint by state officials. In the continuity of blacks in crisis amid the discontinuity of ecological and manufactured disaster crises, will it matter if we are called "Americans" rather than "refugees"? When and where is nation-state membership a passport that possesses tangible value in terms of mobility and survivability, a value that state and civil society must respect for bodies first and foremost recognized as black and impoverished rather than *human*? And who or what can demand, maintain, and enforce that respect when it has been denied?

Struck by and drawn to the voices of historical black mothers trying to keep their children alive and healthy in earlier eras, I hear the continuity of contempt for black humanity amid the discontinuity of epochal disaster and warfare and the continuity of resistance. In Ida B. Wells and Mamie Till-Mobley, a literacy and voice encourage hope and struggle for viability and independence despite institutions that promote premature death and misery through neglect and punishment. Ancestral voices are able to give a literacy that comprehends death edicts coded as law-and-order mandates to be something other than isolated phenomena. The voices of past radicals provide a legibility that enables us to read and then act against the mapping of oppression onto our everyday and extraordinary realities.

State-sanctioned death and dying, overkill for the black frame, have historically been features of US official and unofficial policies towards racially fashioned subjects, the stated or understated enemies to be contained at home and abroad. Policing rhetoric and practices include the visceral: scarred black civilian bodies from the murderous force used in the Danzinger Bridge tragedy, in which police engaged in a shooting spree of innocents as they sought snipers; self-deputized posses, white citizens grinning as they describe to Spike Lee, on tape, their stockpiled weapons for shooting (black) people in order to protect their property (Lee questions, after hearing the gun inventory, if the homeowners are hunting for Bin Laden).

We have heard and seen this before, hence the familiarity to some. Centuries-old grammar books of resistance document the hunter and the prey. Yet when I traveled to New Orleans, I was floored to see the new forms of policing and containment, despite the historical memory and meaning of earlier activists and writers that shaped my ability to read and speak.

southern horrors

When Howard, a former member of the New York City chapter of the Black Panther Party, drove me through the Lower Ninth Ward in March 2006, I saw how 21st-century traumas evoke 19th-century terrors. In the Lower Ninth, post-Reconstruction lynching described in *Southern Horrors* resurfaces. Here, though, only clothes flutter in tree limbs.[3] Here, the dead haven't left bodies behind, to be cut down and buried, to shock the living into mourning. Here is just the suggestion of departed frames, in shirtsleeves and pants legs swaying in breezes or hanging limply from branches, clothing not retrieved months or years after they rooted in the trees of the Lower Ninth. Can there be lynching without a formalized lynch party? Is Billie Holiday's "strange fruit" the predictable harvest from an apartheid city-state left with paltry resources, whose impoverished and outcast have been left to die?

Survivors straggle back by any means necessary to a beloved city, where the majority outside of institutional power never traveled from home, to counter the narrative that they were strung up and are dispossessed. They may read not only a history of repression and resistance into themselves (recalling when levees were "blown up" in earlier eras) but themselves into history (as black New Orleans registers as one of the eviscerating moments of recognition—a fast-forward blur of shared identities through slave codes mutating into black codes and Jim Crow, lynching, the convict prison lease system and current prison mandates)—the historical legacy of black expendability amid racial, economic, and political exclusion.

In March, when Howard pointed out that the exterior walls of homes, propped up on or pushed off of their foundations, had been turned into tombstones by police agencies, funeral markers in the absence of funerals, I had to read again. *Not the absence of agency, agency existed: people were resourceful, found their loved ones, tended the traumatized, buried the dead, worked to rebuild lives and communities.* Radical literacy is not a victim narrative or a mere lamentation; so what was underneath what the police had written on the walls?

I read policing mechanisms that sought to destabilize black agency and autonomy, while constructing graveyards to serve as a staging ground for real estate emptied of "undesirables." So, the NOPD (New Orleans Police Department), the TFW (Texas, Fish and Wildlife), the National Guard, and others spray-painted an acronym, the alleged date of entry into the building, the number of those found alive, the number of dead bodies retrieved, and then encased their quartered codes with a circle to be read clockwise. The deeper we drove into the Ninth, the more painted funeral markers, absent funerals that dignified death, and the longer the wait time before "help" came. The waters came in August 2005, but the state did not, at least for the Ninth Ward. While Howard drove slowly through neighborhoods, I began to see entry dates for the 9th, the 10th, then the 12th months of that year. Mourners from the Ninth Ward would say later that the colorful police tags and graffiti were part truth and part fiction: Police claimed to check homes that they never entered, as unfortunate relatives later discovered when they found unrecognizable corpses.

If the state waits until months after the waters recede, why (claim to) enter at all? Is this a performance of accountability and care? Surely the pretense of rescue takes place on stage, while the concreteness of relief is tossed to private charities or outraged activists and compassionate individuals or resilient people who claim New Orleans as their own: birthplace, hometown, future. The "rescue" or abandonment of the living and/or the remains of those who met or failed to meet the tests are determined by federal, state, and local entities (tests included makeshift levees, tepid warning systems, early non-mandatory evacuation orders, denial of public transportation out of a flood zone and disaster area, and the militarization of humanitarian relief and social stability).

Perhaps in the private graveyards of homes, or the larger graveyards of the most disenfranchised sector of the city, state officials and employees opted for a "closed casket" approach to human suffering—to not witness or at least claim to have not witnessed. In doing so, public servants repeatedly failed their own test, as well as the test for political loyalty and allegiance they demanded from the literate, despite our varied ideologies, and the illiterate (such failures, at home and abroad, have an impact on national elections).

Half a century after Wells wrote her liberation manifesto, and half a century before we began writing what we discerned was "underneath" Katrina, Till-Mobley had an open casket funeral for her son Emmett. She did so for a reason. Defying the injunction by Mississippi police to keep the coffin sealed, and their lining it with lye to hasten the disappearance of the returning teen—defying even the black mortician, who, against her wishes not to alter the face of a mutilated boy, stitched his mouth closed and removed his severed eyes from the sockets—she made him reappear as political and personal trauma. Miss Till-Mobley placed her son on display and dared the world to punish her for publicly mourning and raging against this assault. If we could watch this—rage and grief turning devoted mother momentarily into outlaw (and later into an icon for national embrace), then we could witness, and participate in, the start of a freedom movement. Months before Miss Rosa sat down, Emmett floated, and then putrid and floating was reclaimed, and resurrected, some say through a mother's love turned to hate, to galvanize a movement when thousands attended his funeral in Chicago and tens of thousands witnessed him in his casket in the black press.

Perhaps we have been able to look in the casket to see the alien, and wonder why it looks so familiar, so close, despite the nonhuman and terrifying appearance. Some imagine that that mutilated boy's body was and is part of our legacy, our vulnerability, a sign of ancestors, living kin and community, and future born. As well, some pass on that literacy, become the kind of parent or communicator that would bring a child before an open casket and hold their hand while saying "look"— and look with them. To translate trauma into educational development seems a necessity for those designated to social death by dominant elites and political economies and granted a privileged place for premature physical death from governments that neither protect nor serve. To look into a city turned coffin and see more than police or social/drug violence, dysfunctional governments using incompetence to excuse elites of complicity in violent and premature death for disenfranchised communities, is an act of political literacy.[4]

Look into the casket, as the *Jet* photographer did fifty years ago, and then turn trauma (by proxy) into hope and a massive struggle and fight for life and a dignified death. Political literacy and voice require that we look and act. Those floating in waters have voices amplified in an echo chamber built by imperial policies and our own social failings. What is heard is not only disregard for human life, and the proclivity for grave digging, but resistance.

our ground zero

When Kim encourages me to visit New Orleans during spring break in 2006, he tells me early on that New Orleans is "our ground zero." I take my class and watch it disintegrate as I become ill from environmental toxins in the Ninth Ward and shift my attention between the few students who planned to work and contribute and the majority who seek spectacle to acquire the trophies of trauma tourism. Fight trauma tourism, make mistakes, and realize that you can fly over or touch down (as evident in varied arrays of photo opportunities); and that a class is a microcosmic reflection of a campus, a community, and general society. What is different from fly-over or drop-in trauma tourism, and inept organizing and political factionalism on the ground (which harbor their own forms of narcissism) is to recognize humanity as we witness suffering (our own and others) and recognize that underneath spectacle is a spark where empathy and compassion—not sympathy and charity—function as precursors for radical activism. Which might explain why deep emotions, so difficult to come by and sustain, have a value that exceeds words, even those of transformative literacy.

endnote

1   Ida B. Wells, *Southern Horrors and Other Writings: The Anti-Lynching Campaign of Ida B. Wells, 1892–1900*, ed. Jacqueline Jones Royster (Boston: Bedford Press, 1997), 160.
2   Robert Caldwell, "New Orleans: The Making of an Urban Catastrophe," *MR Zine*, December 9, 2005, http://mrzine. monthlyreview.org/caldwell120905.html.
3   Wells, *Southern Horrors*.
4   There are always counter-narratives seeking to undermine or question literacy: claims to non-racism as an acquisition that absolves rather than attachments to justice through antiracism as labor against racial supremacy and its genocidal logic. Secretaries of state Condoleezza Rice and Colin Powell, copresidents Bush and Dick Cheney inform that the president and government care about (black) people. Reassurances fail as public officials publicly wish for urban ethnic cleansing, fund forced relocation programs, and dispersals turn into disappearance and the denial of the right to return.

    The pre-flood time of a black city marked by impoverishment, disenfranchisement, neglect, corruption, police brutality, and social violence, as well as the commoditization of black culture for consumers, has been noted by activists and scholars. During the flood period, print and electronic media documented the national indifference or aversion toward environmental restoration of wetlands, funding for levees that do not buckle, the incompetence or hostility of federal agencies and relief organizations such as the Army Corps of Engineers, Federal Emergency Management Agency, and the Red Cross. In the post-flood phase, struggles focus on the right of return for the under-resourced and largely black communities, that is, for the right of children to return with their parents, for partners and families to be reunited. To have homes in adequate and safe infrastructures and healthy environments requires massive material support as well as counseling for post-trauma grief and rage. At the same time, many in the United States desire nothing more than political amnesia.

on refuge and language
suheir hammad

I do not wish
To place words in living mouths
Or bury the dead dishonorably

I am not deaf to cries escaping shelters
That citizens are not refugees
Refugees are not Americans

I will not use language
One way or another
To accommodate my comfort

I will not look away

All I know is this

No peoples ever choose to claim status of dispossessed
No peoples want pity above compassion
No enslaved peoples ever called themselves slaves

What do we pledge allegiance to?

A government that leaves its old
To die of thirst surrounded by water
Is a foreign government

People who are streaming
Illiterate into paperwork

Have long ago been abandoned

I think of coded language
And all that words carry on their backs

I think of how it is always the poor
Who are tagged and boxed with labels
Not of their own choosing

I think of my grandparents
And how some called them refugees
Others called them non-existent
They called themselves landless
Which means homeless

Before the hurricane
No tents were prepared for the fleeing
Because Americans do not live in tents
Tents are for Haiti for Bosnia for Rwanda

Refugees are the rest of the world

Those left to defend their human decency
Against conditions the rich keep their animals from
Those who have too many children
Those who always have open hands and empty bellies
Those whose numbers are massive
Those who seek refuge
From nature's currents and man's resources

Those who are forgotten in the mean times

Those who remember

Ahmad from Guinea makes my falafel sandwich and says
So this is your country

Yes Amadou this my country

And these my people

Evacuated as if criminal
Rescued by neighbors
Shot by soldiers

Adamant they belong

The rest of the world can now see
What I have seen

Do not look away

The rest of the world lives here too
In America

acknowledgments

We first raise a glass to the contributors. Your willingness to get on board and make this book happen truly felt like solidarity in action. You never turned off your porch light and pretended not to be home. In the struggle for a better world, we're proud to be in it with you.

We'd like to give shout outs to many behind the scenes folks: copyeditor Erich Strom and proofreader Esther Dwinell, your funny editorial remarks, nuanced queries, and ability to cope with rolling rush deadlines just made it all better; indexer and ad hoc proofreader Chris Dodge, your last minute finds were invaluable; Innosanto Nagara and William Ramírez and their fellow artists/warriors at Design Action Collective, collective process—holla! Annie Deziel at Transcon and Nicole Baxter at BookMobile, you're our production angels; our distributor CBSD, the sales reps, and the bookstore buyers for understanding that this project is so much more than a "Katrina" book.

Our beloved interns: Kerry Cardoza, Allie Compton, Lillian DeVane, Val Grimm, Erica Kapitan-Daniel, Alexa Punnamkuzhyil, Timothy Rodes, Wolf Seiler, Alex Straaik, Beatrice Sullivan, Gabriela Suau, and Edmund Townsend. You all do so much for us. We'd be hurtin' for certain without you.

You know why: Mumia Abu Jamal, Mario Africa, Amiri Baraka, Irene Castagliola, Jeff Chang, Raymond Fiore, Glen Ford, Jeremy Glick, bell hooks, Joy James, Robert Jensen, Margaret Kimberley, Tamara K. Nopper, Vijay Prashad, Vandana Shiva, Barbara Smith, Frank B. Wilderson III, Nancy Yap, and Howard Zinn.

We feel weird saying this, but we'd each like to thank the rest of the collective (Joey, Jocelyn, Asha, Alexander, Jill). As this book shows, it's important to say the things that often go unspoken.

Most of all, we dedicate this book to the people directly affected by the storm. We hope it honors in some small way the memory of those who died—and stands in support of those who remain and continue to fight for their right to return, for their recognition as stakeholders, and for that better world.

roger benham is a certified Wilderness Emergency Medical Technician-Basic and action medic. Among other things, he's been a park ranger, motel clerk, theater tech, and beekeeper, and currently works at a nontraditional home for autistic adults in the forests of the Quinnebaug-Shetucket bioregion, "the last green valley" between Boston and New York City. He lives in Willimantic, Connecticut, with his wife Heather and a fierce cat named Caldera. When not searching for the resurgent New England mountain lion, he dj's a country music show on community radio, reads too much, and longs to return to New Orleans.

alisa bierria is a radical Black feminist and is on the national steering committee of INCITE! Women of Color Against Violence. Alisa, her family, and her ancestors are from New Orleans, and she is helping to support the extraordinary work of local women of color there. She currently goes to school in California where she is developing a philosophical framework to describe agency as it exists in the context of oppression.

tiffany brown is the Center for AIDS Research Community Advisory Board Coordinator at the University of Pennsylvania. Tiffany conducts research projects focusing on HIV/AIDS addressing such topics as the connection between HIV and IV drug use; how depression effects disease progression; and an experimental HIV vaccine. Additionally, she is a Black Youth Vote organizer and spends time mobilizing young adults around issues of voter education and participation, environmental justice, and youth homelessness. Tiffany was raised in New Orleans and moved to Philadelphia in 1997. She has a series of poetry published by Thoughts In Black, Incorporated.

mandy carter is a self-described "southern out black lesbian social justice activist." She has worked in multiracial and multi-issue grassroots organizing for the last 37 years. Her introduction to activism happened in the late 1960's through the Quaker-based American Friends Service Committee, the pacifist-based War Resisters League, and the former Institute for the Study of Nonviolence. Since then, she has worked with the National Black Justice Coalition, Southerners On New Ground, Gay and Lesbian Advocates and Defenders, and the Freedom to Marry Collaborative, as well as serving as a Member-At-Large of the Democratic National Committee, among many, many other progressive, social justice organizations.

scott crow is an anarchist community organizer, trainer and writer who began working on anti-apartheid, and animal rights issues in the mid 1980s. He cofounded and co-organized Common Ground Relief, UPROAR (United People Resisting Oppression and Racism), Radical Encuentro Camp, and North Texas Coalition for a Just Peace. He has trained and organized for Greenpeace, Ruckus Society, ACORN and many smaller grassroots groups. scott co-produced a documentary about the Angola 3 and is currently collaborating on long-term, sustainable, democratic, economic projects within Austin.

lisa fithian has been working for social change since the mid 1970's. She has been a student, labor and community organizer on a broad range of issues from environmental justice and worker rights to peace and global justice issues. Lisa has worked for over a year in organizing relief efforts with the Common Ground Collective in New Orleans. Common Ground's efforts have been a culmination of Lisa's long-term work confronting racism, corporate greed and a lack of government accountability while building sustainable alternatives to the current social structure. Lisa Fithian is 45 years old and lives in Austin, Texas.

jordan flaherty is a writer and community organizer based in New Orleans. His articles from the Gulf Coast after Hurricane Katrina have appeared in periodicals around the world, including Germany's *Die Zeit*, *Clarin* in Argentina, *Juventude Rebelde* in Cuba, and *Red Pepper* in England. In the US, his articles have appeared in a wide range of publications from *ColorLines* to *The Village Voice* to several anthologies and literally hundreds of blogs and web-based journals including *ZNet*, *CommonDreams*, *AlterNet* and *Counterpunch*. He is an editor of *Left Turn*, a magazine of globalized resistance.

ross gelbspan was a reporter and editor for 31 years at *The Philadelphia Bulletin*, *The Washington Post* and *The Boston Globe*. Following his retirement from daily journalism, he published *The Heat Is On: the Climate Crisis, the Cover-Up, the Prescription* in 1998, which he followed up in 2004 with the publication of *Boiling Point*, one of the top science books of 2004, according to *Discover Magazine*. His articles on the climate issue have appeared in *Harper's Magazine*, *The Atlantic Monthly*, *The Nation* and *The American Prospect*. Gelbspan lives in Brookline, Massachusetts, with his wife, Anne, and two daughters, Thea and Johanna.

shana griffin is a black feminist single mother that grew up in a racially and economically segregated public housing development in downtown New Orleans, where she became acutely aware of economic, racial, and gender disparities fueled by violence and the over-policing of communities of color. Shana currently serves on the national steering committee of INCITE! Women of Color Against Violence and is also an active member of INCITE! New Orleans. Shana is also co-producing a documentary on the Louisiana State Chapter of the Black Panther Party, and is conducting research for a black women's film project.

suheir hammad was born in Amman, Jordan to Palestinian refugee parents on October 25, 1973. Suheir's family immigrated to Brooklyn when she was five years old, and she was raised there until the age of sixteen. Suheir has been able to travel throughout the world via her poetry. She has read her poems in Ivy League Universities and on Brooklyn's street corners. As far as we know, Suheir was the first Palestinian starring in a Broadway show, and she continues to be the first Palestinian in many artistic spaces throughout the States.

sue hilderbrand is an activist and community organizer, educator and traveler. Her activism has focused mostly on corporate globalization and war. She spent two years as a Peace Corps volunteer in Morocco and has traveled extensively across several continents. She currently teaches political science courses at a community college in northern California.

incite! women of color against violence is a national activist organization of radical feminists of color advancing a movement to end violence against women of color and their communities through direct action, critical dialogue, and grassroots organizing. The New Orleans chapter of INCITE! is a collective of local women of color that is building powerful mechanisms for facilitating women's access to safety and health care as it builds a political base for revolutionary change. For more information about our work and mission, including how to get involved, please visit www.incite-national.org or contact us at incite_national@yahoo.com.

joy james is the John B. and John T. McCoy Presidential Professor of Africana Studies and College Professor in Political Science at Williams College, where she chairs the Africana Studies program. She is the author of *Resisting State Violence and Shadowboxing: Representations of Black Feminist Politics*. Her edited collections on radical politics and incarceration include: *Imprisoned Intellectuals*; *The New Abolitionists*; and *Warfare in the American Homeland: Policing and Prison in a Penal Democracy*.

lewis lapham is editor emeritus of *Harper's Magazine*, for which he writes a monthly essay called "Notebook." He won a 1995 National Magazine Award for three of those essays, in which the judges discovered "an exhilarating point of view in an age of conformity."

ricardo levins morales is a visual artist, labor activist, and social movement strategist. He was born in the coffee growing mountains of western Puerto Rico and developed his art as part of his activism in grassroots political movements, beginning at age thirteen. Since 1979 he has been a member of the Northland Poster Collective in Minneapolis, Minnesota, which provides artistic support to social change struggles.

mayaba liebenthal is a black feminist, anarchist, human rights advocate and community organizer committed to creating projects/ institutions that support self-determined and sustainable community development. A New Orleans resident, she has been involved in community organizing projects relating to gender-violence, media justice, law enforcement violence, prison abolition, and affordable housing. She is a member of various community based organizations including, the New Orleans chapter of INCITE! Women of Color Against Violence, Critical Resistance, Nowe Miasto, and the Public Digital Urban Broadcasters (public DUB).

charmaine neville is a member of the third generation of New Orleans' legendary Neville musical family. She fronts the Charmaine Neville Band. This is a transcript of an interview she gave to a variety of media outlets on Monday, September 5, 2005.

ewuare osayande (www.osayande.org) is a poet and political activist. The author of several books including *Blood Luxury* (Africa World Press), he is cofounder of POWER (People Organized Working to Eradicate Racism) based in Philadelphia.

malik rahim is a veteran of the Black Panther Party in New Orleans, a long time housing and prison activist, and a recent Green Party candidate for New Orleans City Council. He lives in the Algiers neighborhood of New Orleans.

dylan rodríguez is an Associate Professor at the University of California at Riverside. Dylan is an interdisciplinary scholar-activist whose interests traverse the fields of critical race studies and cultural studies, with focal attention to the intersections of race, state violence, and community/identity formation. His first book, *Forced Passages: Imprisoned Radical Intellectuals and the U.S. Prison Regime* was published in 2006 and his writings have appeared in many scholarly journals. A founding member of the Critical Resistance organizing collective, Dylan is proudly and critically engaged with a variety of progressive and radical movements and political formations.

kalamu ya salaam (kalamu@aol.com) is codirector of Students at the Center, an independent writing program that works within New Orleans public high schools. Salaam teaches creative writing and digital video. He is also the director of the Listen to the People oral history project, which consists of video interviews with over 30 individuals including activists from the black, white, Latino, and Vietnamese communities, as well as the various social classes within the New Orleans Black community. More information about his work is available at www.kalamu.com.

jared sexton, Ph.D., teaches in the Program in African American Studies and the Department of Film and Media Studies at the University of California, Irvine. He is the author most recently of *Amalgamation Schemes: Antiblackness and the Critique of Multiracialism* (University of Minnesota Press, forthcoming) as well as various scholarly articles and book chapters.

about the **people's hurricane relief fund and oversight coalition**

Hurricane Katrina put a spotlight on the horrors of racism, sexism, national oppression, poverty, and environmental destruction in the US. After the hurricane, when it became clear that the US government was not going to help the displaced communities—in particular the black and other oppressed communities of the Gulf Coast—hurt by the storm, the People's Hurricane Relief Fund and Oversight Coalition was born. Community organizers and concerned people acknowledged that we must hold accountable those who abandoned us and that those of us most adversely affected should have a central role in all aspects of putting our lives back together, individually and collectively.

The purpose of People's Hurricane Relief is to ensure a grassroots hurricane-survivors' movement that allows people from New Orleans and the Gulf Coast region to play a central role in all decisions made about relief and the rebuilding of the area. This movement is meant to be a people's movement—a movement made up of the persons disproportionately impacted by Hurricane Katrina and the dehumanizing treatment of local, state, and federal officials. We are committed to ensuring mechanisms by which those who want to return home to New Orleans and the Gulf Coast are able to, regardless of economic, geographical, or citizenship status prior to displacement.

We seek to build and maintain a coordinated network of survivors, community leaders, organizers, and community-based organizations with the capacity and organizational infrastructure needed to help win the demands of those who were most affected by the storm. To that end, we facilitate the return and rebuilding process while empowering local, grassroots leadership with national and international support. Our organization also fosters oppressed nationality leadership, particularly black leadership, with the support of a multinational alliance. People's Hurricane Relief places special emphasis on the involvement of women, oppressed nationalities, poor, gay, lesbian, queer, and transgender populations, immigrants, indigenous, youth, and people with disabilities.

For more information, updates, or details on our current programming focus, please visit www.peopleshurricane.org, call (504) 301-0215, email phrfoc@gmail.com, or write 1418 N. Claiborne Ave. #2, New Orleans, LA 70116.

about south end press

South End Press is an independent, collectively run book publisher with more than 250 titles in print. Since our founding in 1977, we have met the needs of readers who are exploring, or are already committed to, the politics of radical social change. We publish books that encourage critical thinking and constructive action on the key political, cultural, social, economic, and ecological issues shaping life in the United States and in the world. We provide a forum for a wide variety of democratic social movements and an alternative to the products of corporate publishing.

From its inception, South End has organized itself as an egalitarian collective with decision-making arranged to share as equally as possible the rewards and stresses of running the business. Each collective member is responsible for core editorial and administrative tasks, and all collective members earn the same base salary. South End also has made a practice of inverting the pervasive racial and gender hierarchies in traditional publishing houses; our collective has been majority women since the mid-1980s, and at least 50 percent people of color since the mid-1990s.

Our author list—which includes bell hooks, Andrea Smith, Arundhati Roy, Noam Chomsky, Winona LaDuke, Manning Marable, Ward Churchill, Cherríe Moraga, and Howard Zinn—reflects South End's commitment to publish on myriad issues from diverse perspectives.

community supported publishing

Celebrate the bounty of the book harvest! Community Supported Agriculture is helping to make independent, healthy farming sustainable. Now there is CSP! By joining the South End Press CSP, you ensure a steady crop of books guaranteed to change your world. As a member you receive one of the new varieties or a choice heirloom selection free each month and a 10% discount on everything else. Subscriptions start at $20/month. Email southend@ southendpress.org for more details.

read. write. revolt.